Contact

Also by Janusz Wrobel

Language and Schizophrenia
(1990, Amsterdam & Philadelphia)

Polska po polsku [Poland in Polish]:
A Polish Language Handbook for Beginners
(1986, Warsaw)

IN POLISH

Papers from the Second Congress
of the Scholars of Polish Origin
(co-edited with H. Kubiak)
(1984, Warsaw & Krakow)

Cztery pory tutaj [Four Seasons Here]: Selected Poems
(Siedlce, 2008)

Poczekalnia [A Waiting Room]: Selected Poems
(Detroit, 1996)

Contact

The Tale of Human Longing For Fulfilling Communication

Janusz Wrobel

Wisdom Moon Publishing
2013

CONTACT:
THE TALE OF HUMAN LONGING
FOR FULFILLING COMMUNICATION

Copyright © 2013 Wisdom Moon Publishing, LLC
All rights reserved. Tous droits réservés.

No part of this work may be copied, reproduced, recorded, stored, or translated, in any form, or transmitted by any means electronic, mechanical, or other, whether by photocopy, fax, email, internet group postings, or otherwise, without written permission from the copyright holder, *except for brief quotations* in reviews for a magazine, journal, newspaper, broadcast, podcast, etc., or in scholarly or academic papers, *when quoted with a full citation to this work.*

Published by Wisdom Moon Publishing LLC
San Diego, CA, USA

Wisdom Moon™, the Wisdom Moon logo™, *Wisdom Moon Publishing*™, and *WMP*™ are trademarks of Wisdom Moon Publishing LLC.

www.WisdomMoonPublishing.com

ISBN 978-1-938459-31-3 (softcover, alk. paper)
ISBN 978-1-938459-38-2 (eBook)
LCCN 2013956832

Front cover image by Julie Jalil, "After Mitchev" (2004), Oil and Gold Leaf on Canvas, www.JalilArt.com.

Photography by Andrei Ciortan, andrei.ciortan@gmail.com.

For those who are led and strengthened by the illusion of contact.

All words [kol ha-d'varim] are tiresome, one can no longer speak; the eye is not satisfied with seeing, nor the ear fulfilled with hearing.
Ecclesiastes 1:8

Words are the source of misunderstandings.
Antoine de Saint-Exupéry

Contents

Prologue   i

First Longing: Contact with Reality   1

Why *Chair* Requires Context
The World and the Word, or How Far, How Close?
What Do We Lose When We Get Language?
World According to Grenouille
The Idols of Francis Bacon
The World and the Personal World
The Very Personal World and the World

Second Longing: Contacts with Others   19
"A Soft Tongue Breaketh the Bone"
Understanding, or, when I Mean What You Think I Mean
Lack of Understanding, or, Superiority of Common Speech
Misunderstanding One Another, or, What I (incorrectly) Think
      You Think vs. What You (incorrectly) Think I Think
Conditions of a Successful Speech Act
What Does the Human Face Communicate?
A Word on Electronic Communication

Third Longing: Contact between Her and Him   35
A Beautiful Angel of Death
Time and the Landscape of Memory
The Ultimate Exchange
Freedom and Roles to Be Played.
Loneliness of the Two
Communication without Contact
The Undisclosed and the Irretrievable Contacts

Fourth Longing: Contact with Strangers   49
Total Inadequacy
Identity Crisis, or, Not HERE, Not NOW; Who Am I?
Value Crisis and Communication Crisis: The East/Central
      European Case Study
The Four Ways of Dealing with the Immigrant Experience

Adjusting to the New Country
Peripheries of Contact: War and Occupation
New Walls in People's Hearts or
    Hope Isn't That Young Girl Anymore...

Fifth Longing: Contact with Yourself   67
The Curse of Egohood
Uniqueness and Unity: The Two Basic Longings
"I Doubt Nothing but the Certainties"
The Beautiful Uncertainty
What Does the Unpredictable Have to Do With Freedom?
Prisoners of Polarity
Contradictions and a Rain-charmer
And what if *Contraria sunt complementa*?
Where Does the Robin's Tail Reside? (From the Perspective
    of a Grain of Sand)

Epilogue   89

References   91

Acknowledgments   97

PROLOGUE

The human being has been described in many ways. Some would suggest that the main feature of human nature is its social inclination: that a person is a social being and that the most eminent feature of human nature is a desperate attempt to communicate.

Here, a person will be described as a communicative creature whose main aims are to become a fully emotional being, to create new physical and spiritual realities, to express himself, and to have significant interactions involving ongoing exchanges with others. I believe that one of the major meanings of life lies in communicating—what one gives to the world and what one absorbs from it—in the process of these eternal exchanges. The ultimate exchange occurs in love, but our discussion will be extended to various additional kinds of communicative interactions.

The essence of successful communication is contact. Longing for contact drives us when we begin to talk, write, draw, play an instrument, compose, or perform. All these activities are expressive, but the ultimate goal of those who undertake them is to touch others' lives through the means of expressive tools. For a speaker, a writer, an artist, a musician, a composer, or an actress, the most important feat is to reach an audience. Supposedly, some writers intend to keep their creation in a drawer, and some artists claim they do not need an audience, but by some coincidence, those are usually the same artists who have trouble being published or discovered.

Commencing one's creation, one has in mind a prospective receiver of one's effort. One can take into consideration common taste and the receiver's expectations or not, but even when creating so-called pure art—art for the sake of art—it is always addressed to those who share common taste; in basic terms, one strives for an understanding recipient of the message. The personal dream is to address at least one other human being with whom sharing a reciprocal understanding would be possible. The act of mutual accord between the one who sends some message and the one who accurately understands it, I will call contact.

Some selected channels of communication have been mentioned, but I will also discuss many others, from the ultimate reciprocal communication, which is love, to the most destructive form of communication, which is war. Here, communication is meant in rather broad sense of *exchange* between one human being and other human beings, but also between humankind and mainly, but not exclusively, the elements of surrounding reality.

The most common communicative tool is language, thus I will mainly deal with this major instrument of exchange among people, putting special emphasis on the causes of imperfection in language communication. One of the most frequent themes in this book is this communicative, perception-defined constraint that limits our contacts and acquirable knowledge.

Communicative exchange is such an important part of our life and refers to so many features of our activities that it probably would be easier to specify what is not communication, instead of trying to indicate what belongs to the communicative processes.

Most human activity is, in a certain measure, based on communicative exchange. We are either in the stage of exchanging messages (sending or receiving them), in the stage of anticipating them, or in the stage of interpreting them. What distinguishes us from the surrounding animated world is not that we exchange information, but our relentless desire to establish a contact through this exchange—to understand and to be understood.

Of course, this book is a reflection of my own experiences in addition to my observations and the projection of my own beliefs, cultural background and limitations that come from my gender, race, and age. I had not been sure how to explain this framework of my writing to my prospective readers until I read a statement of Thomas Moore in the Preface to his book *Soul Mates* (1994). I believe that what he wrote there reflects my feelings so exactly that I have decided to quote his words here:

> *I'm also aware that I write as a white, male, heterosexual American with a classical European education, and that many who will read these words do not share that background. While writing, I've tried to maintain some consciousness of these potential differences, but to do so at very turn is to become so self-conscious and contorted as to lose touch with my own experience, which is an important source of my reflections. So I ask the reader to allow me to speak from my*

own context. I hope that what I say from my experience will apply, with reservations and sometimes with substantive changes, to various other arrangements and other cultural and educational backgrounds.

T. Moore, *Soul Mates*, 1994, pp. vii-viii.

FIRST LONGING:
CONTACT WITH REALITY
(FROM SYMBIOSIS TO DICHOTOMY)

Why *Chair* requires context

Technically speaking, language consists of words that when combined according to grammatical rules create phrases and sentences. Words, from this perspective, are the smallest independent meaningful units of language.

Let us consider one expression among all the words, the term *a chair*. When we hear or read this phrase, we may understand that *a chair* here could mean (a) *moveable seat for one with a back,* (b) *person in charge of a meeting,* (c) *position of a university professor,* or (d) *the electric chair*. Our choice among these options in any given context will depend on additional available information.

The context in which our term appears will probably allow us to eliminate three out of the four meanings here. In fact, the process of elimination was started even before we took the mentioned meanings into consideration: the determiner 'a' (in the phrase here, 'a chair') indicated that we dealt with a noun; thus, an additional optional verbal meaning, *act as chairman of some group,* was eliminated immediately.

The additional information I referred to can be delivered by the context of other words in which our *chair* appears, e.g., the expression "what a comfortable chair" would indicate an object rather than a person; on the other hand, the statement "The chair enthusiastically encouraged me in the meeting" would imply to us, instead, a person. Essential context can be brought, however, by other indicators: the term *chair* proclaimed in a furniture store will direct our choice of meaning in a different direction than the same word pronounced in the presence of a group of scholars representing different departments of the same university.

Let us agree that in some context we have obtained enough indicators to decide that the relevant meaning is: *a moveable seat for one*. We know now that the object is a piece of furniture, but unless we see the specific one, a set of images of different chairs might appear in our minds. This stage of meaning-analysis will awaken associations connected with a concept of a chair. Two main groups of associations will appear: the one commonly shared with the users of language, and a private one, pertaining to individual listeners. The former, lexical, will represent different kinds of chairs we have learned of: wooden, plastic, metal, garden, royal, armchair, kitchen, etc.; the latter, emotional, will bring to our minds sentiments we have in connection with particular chairs in our lives.

Emotions will add nuances to our understanding; they will personalize it. This is the moment of the first serious impact of subjective experiences on our understanding. Let us imagine that someone had inherited a chair from somebody with whom he had been in a close personal relationship; or, let us think about someone who had a family member who spent his life in a wheel-chair, about someone who paid a fortune for a Louis XIV chair, only to discover later that he had bought a well-made forgery, about someone who after all these years still remembers his high-chair in which he was imprisoned till he would eat everything that was served to him, or about someone who will always miss her toy chair that had been unceremoniously thrown out by her parents during a move.

Let us think about these possible individualizations and maybe some seemingly incomprehensible reactions witnessed by us during conversations with some people will become more meaningful. U.S. Supreme Court Justice Oliver Wendell Holmes once said, "*A word is not a crystal, transparent and unchanged, it is the skin of a living thought and may vary greatly in color and content according to the circumstances and the time in which it is used.*" (Towne v. Eisner, 245 U.S. 418, 1918.)

Returning now to our *chair:* thanks to necessary contextual and spatial references, the one who heard this word was able to comprehend it. She individualized it a little bit, but a basic concept of a chair as *a moveable seat for one* was understood. In this way, we can say that in this imaginary context, the one who said the word and the other, who understood it, understood it in this same way. At the level of this single word, communicative success was gained.

While celebrating this comprehension, we should have in our minds that the idea of a chair belongs to the class of rather simple, substantive concepts. Speculative (more abstract) concepts, on the other hand, can cause more subtle and more important complications in our desire for communication.

Love, for instance, is semantically so rich a term that to understand properly what was meant by a speaker, we need assistance from additional adjectives, nouns, or verbs, to narrow the meaning of it, allowing us to refer, e.g., to *a mother's love, a girlfriend's love, love of country*, or *love of money*. Without such additions, we would not be able to obtain the proper meaning.

The richness of these various individual associations connected with the term in focus means that prospective communicative misunderstanding is much more probable than in the case of semantically less-loaded words (like 'chair'). When it comes to this particular term, a language user already has a concrete sense of it in his mind; this is not the case of the idea of love. We may have many distinct interpretations and associations of this idea in our minds, depending on its contextual significance.

The context may bring totally new and unexpected meaning to terms that otherwise had quite fixed associational meanings. Let us consider the term *Stanford University,* for instance. In a common understanding, this term is associated with a prestigious institution of higher education that is offering excellence in teaching. This particular meaning obviously was not on mind of a four-year old girl who stated in her preschool in Palo Alto, California, that she had started to save money for the sake of studying at *Stanford University*. When asked why at *Stanford University*, she answered: "Students do not have to take an afternoon nap there." In this way, a new, contextual meaning of *Stanford University* was created: *a school in Stanford, California, where students have more freedom than in the Palo Alto preschool.*

Another illustration of a new, unexpected understanding of a term is found in a playful message from NASA HQ in Houston, where at the end of a conversation with the astronauts returning from their moon mission to Earth, their terrestrial associates played for them an Elvis Presley song, "Return to Sender"—here the "sender" was not the person who mailed the letter of the lyrics, but NASA, which had sent the astronauts on their mission in the first place.

The possibility of ambiguity of words' meanings and significance leads us sometimes to confusion even when a context is available. The following refers to my personal experience: *The Detroit Free Press* on March 19, 1993, published an article by

Roddy Ray that was titled "A Low Scam In Hungary: Scheme sells worms, wipes out savings, leads to suicides."

The title and then the beginning of the article that depicts a series of suicides in Hungary caused by earthworms challenged not only that part of my self-esteem that deals with my comprehension of English but even, though for seconds only, my common sense. I thought, "Either I have gone insane, or the author has." I continued my reading still suspecting that the term 'earthworm' has in English a second or idiomatic meaning, unknown to me. At this moment, I checked in all dictionaries in my office. The more I read, the more the literal meaning became clearer to me. True, according to the article, many Hungarians invested bank credits in purchasing huge amounts of worms, that when reproduced were to be sold to somebody else with an obvious profit. What is more, the selling company was to buy the worms' waste, as a valuable fertilizer. As unfortunate investors quickly discovered, they were neither able to sell anything, nor to pay off costly credits. Some of those entrepreneurs decided to commit suicide.

This is a story that I feel, considering here its tragic content, should have been written in less sensational form. The author of the article (or in other words, a sender of communication) formulated a message that confused me first, scared me later, and then, because of its specifics, disgusted me. Because it was not possible to talk to the writer of the article, I can only speculate to what extent my reaction, the receiver's reaction, was in accordance to the sender's intentions. The example of this article brings us deeper into the problem of the relationship between the reality we live in or describe (e.g. the earthworm scheme) and the realm of words.

The World and the Word, or How Far, How Close?

You well know that Adonai had created the world and then turned himself into the Word. Word drives air and mind, simultaneously affects senses and souls. Even if you are not initiated, you will be able to reason that the Word is a necessary mediator between the material world and every mind; a spiritual essence of the universe, wrote Jan Potocki in his mystical book, *The Manuscript Found in Saragossa* (vol. 1, pp. 138-139), indicating three elements that participate in the mystery of naming. Those elements are

(a) *what is being named,* or a reality that includes both visible and invisible elements; (b) *a word that gives a name*, the tool of designating, which is here Potocki's intermediary between language and world; (c) *a concept of what was named*, or images or ideas of the reality in our minds. Using our example with "chair," these elements are (a) an actual, physical chair, (b) a set of sounds or letters c-h-a-i-r, and (c) an image or concept of a chair in our minds.

Language equips us with a descriptive tool that allows us to talk about the surrounding world. Words are the representatives of reality; they are transmitters of our impressions about reality, and we use them as we use spoons to eat soup.

Chuang Tzu (or, Zhuangzi, in more contemporary Pinyin transliteration), described the relationship between the tool and the result of action in which the tool is used this way (after Fritjof Capra, *The Tao of Physics*, 1975, p. 28):

> *Fishing baskets are employed to catch fish; but when the fish are got, the men forget the baskets; snares are employed to catch hares; but when the hares are got, men forget the snares. Words are employed to convey ideas; but when the ideas are grasped, men forget the words.*

Words given to us are organized in a certain logical systems and as Alfred Korzybski aptly wrote, they create a map of reality. The imperfection of maps and their inaccuracy in the description of physical space is well known; maps are none the less used despite their limitations, conventionality, and arbitrariness, because there is no better tool. Regardless of a theoretical awareness about its limited effectiveness, we use language with amazing confidence, so much so that it stops fulfilling the role of mediator between us and reality, and begins to replace reality itself in our understanding.

Indian philosophy uses the term *maya (illusion)* to describe a state of confusion experienced by somebody who mixes up reality with its linguistic appearance. Capra (p. 88) explains that the above-mentioned *illusion* does not refer to the world but to our perception:

> *The illusion merely lies in our point of view, if we think that the shapes and structures, things and events, around us are realities of nature, instead of realizing that they are concepts*

of our measuring and categorizing minds. "Maya" is the illusion of taking these concepts for reality, of confusing the map with the territory.

Illustration by Urszula Wrobel.

One of the goals of this book is to offer to its readers some advice in terms of the better use of language. One of the most effective ways for the user of the instrument to improve the performance of it, is to study the nature of the instrument. The more you know about language, the better will be your effectiveness and accuracy in the use of it as a tool that not only describes reality but can also influence it.

What Do We Lose When We Get Language?

It is not known what an infant has in her mind. We can only suspect that the border between the external world and herself is not as significant as it is in the case of the adults. The moment we give language to a child, we help her to identify herself and simultaneously to distinguish herself from the surrounding world. The crucial word here is the term 'I' that basically means *not you, not Mommy, not he, not she, not they, not the world*. In process of learning language, we come to the first oppositions: *I ≠ world*. The first opposition is followed by thousands of others: *good ≠ bad, young ≠ old, pretty ≠ ugly*, etc. Because our language is based on pairs of contradictions, it is said that it has binary (having two distinctive parts) or dichotomous (having two contradictory elements) character.

Of course, reality is more complicated than the binary character of language would suggest. This is why we often face a hopeless task when attempting to describe in mere words the richness, variety, and complexity of our experiences and world. The binary nature of language makes it difficult to talk about certain phenomena, e.g., a child that is yet to be born. The reason for this comes from the "logical inconsistency" in which this term is trapped: a child does exist in mother's womb, but, simultaneously, as an unborn one, does not yet exist. Sometimes a description is used to express this unusual, allegedly contradictory state; a prospective mother is called the "expecting" one. Again, we should mention that from the point of view of logic that feeds language, this term is not very accurate here: 'to expect' refers to something that is yet to occur, and a baby, no doubt about it, has already "occurred." An unborn child lives, moves, grows, hears the voices from the outside word, and "tastes" the food that is eaten by its mother.

The imperfection of our binary communicative tool sometimes forces us into the creation of strangely juxtaposed phrases in order to express associations more sophisticated than the binary relations; thus we order sweet and sour sauce, we talk about the sweet slavery of love, we cannot decide what we feel: hatred or admiration, or maybe both simultaneously, putting into jeopardy our common logic. In thinking about this common logic we may refer back to Francis Bacon, who in his writings used the term 'vulgar' meaning *common*. Our approach here is based on our ambiguity when it comes to deciding what is common about our so-called common logic.

Those who fight with the tyranny of words, driven by their own aspirations toward achieving a true and full contact with nature, know that at some points they have to give up on words as intermediaries. This is when we sense that words are creating a barrier between reality and us, the users of language. Unfortunately, this barrier replaces reality for most careless language-users. The most dramatic form of this phenomenon is observed in schizophrenia, where words take a physical, material dimension and consequently can harm the users in an almost physical way.

The seekers of true contact become mystics, focusing on overcoming the basic dichotomy *I ≠ world* that was given to us by language. In a mystical state, they surrender the element *I* (as representing use of language) in their perception of the world. William Blake, in *There Is No Natural Religion* (1794-95), wrote, *"He who sees the Infinite in all things sees God. He who sees the Ratio only, sees himself only."*

It is not the goal of this book to state definitively that language is exclusively responsible for its users' tendency to perceive certain complex elements of reality through the prism of only two, contradictory extremes. But the impact of our language on process of thinking cannot be denied. Creating a confining, maya-like understanding of reality by imposing two contrasting options is a familiar tactic of those who use language as means of persuasion in order to obtain expected responses, for example, from prospective buyers, or from voters in coming elections. Commercial or political goals are gained by presenting those to whom the messages are directed with a false choice of two possibilities: either happiness brought by the product, or despair caused by the poor quality goods made by the competition; either prosperity promised by the politician, or permanent crisis caused by his opponent. A choice given in such messages is often false and distorting of the reality considered (there being in the context more than the two options being presented as exhaustive of our choices), especially in advertising and in the language of propaganda, demagoguery, and populism.

The mature user of language is more familiar with this, more aware, and more skeptical about such techniques; younger or more naïve individuals are easier targets for this sort of manipulation. Such people have a tendency to be uncritical, impulsive, sharp, and, accepting of such binary options, are more convinced by their weak reasoning.

Being mature often means that our perception of reality becomes more complex and sophisticated. More and more often, we comprehend that between black and white there are many shades of gray. Lack of understanding of this phenomenon is a significant source of misunderstandings.

Let us consider an example here. The context is as follows: a married man was dying in the hospital, he was thinking about his mistress, was longing for her; instead, his unloved wife was standing by his bed. He was not able to shout, to talk, even to whisper; the only thing he could do was to look up at her "with infinite hatred." Meanwhile, his wife knew for sure that

> *she was the only person he asked for. He couldn't talk, but how he'd thanked her with his eyes! He'd fixed his eyes on her and begged to be forgiven. And she forgave him.*
> M. Kundera, *The Unbearable Lightness of Being*,
> 1987, p. 277.

After years of using language, we consider it to be an intrinsic part of our life. Most of the users of this major communicative tool do not remember the significant distinction between reality and its intermediary—language. What is forgotten is its conventional, arbitrary, symbolic, and relative character. Plainly speaking, we do not realize that between the word (letters, spoken word) c-h-a-i-r and a real chair there in nothing but a conventional relationship. Let us imagine that for naming this furniture we use the letters (or spoken word) h-c-i-r-a instead. Is one term more naturally connected with *a moveable seat for one* than the other? Not at all. The relation that we are familiar with is treated as "natural" because of established tradition, the length of use of language, and for the sake of successful communication. We all use the same linguistic symbol for the same object in order to comprehend each other. We could use an arbitrary convention (and so, a different word could be chosen); the relation between words and the world is relative. We can only think about a truly "natural" connection between word and reality in case of onomatopoeic words that imitate certain characteristic sounds, such as *cuckoo, sizzle,* or *hush*. That's why the Zen text, *The Gateless Gate* (p. 159), describes our mind as "dualistic, outgoing, generalizing [and] intellectualizing."

It is difficult to recognize the relative nature of our language. We are oblivious to the fact that we organize our vocabulary according to classifications that were decided through time and experience. How many of us using language remember that we systematize our conceptual, imaginary world in agreement with our personal, emotional, and individual time and spatial relations, using, e.g., the following criteria: "all vacations with Eve," "all vacations with Maggie," "all vacations after winning the lottery." More or less of personal nature, these criteria still remain *relative*. This special attribute of language is of immense importance for those who consider themselves conscious users of this communicative instrument.

The World According to Grenouille

With words, we *create* reality rather than describe it. One of the supporting arguments for this statement might be the numerous and diverse criteria used in systematizing our treasury of words. What's more, the existing guidelines could easily be expanded. For instance, to those mentioned so far might be added one more classifiable criterion: smells.

Imagine: could we categorize features of the world according to our olfactory experience? Impossible? Not for Jean-Baptiste Grenouille, the hero of the story *Das Parfum (Perfume)*, by Patrick Süskind. Grenouille, this teenage boy, despite being mentally challenged and almost completely socially withdrawn, possesses a unique talent: not only he is able to smell what others cannot, but he can distinguish and classify countless subtle and quite nuanced variations of his nasal experiences. For instance, what for an average person was just milk—for Grenouille, this white beverage was divided into several categories according to his olfactory criteria that allowed him to recognize which cow produced it, what kind of food the cow had been exposed to the day before or how much cream it included. Another example pertains to the domain of wood. For this future perfume production's master, just his sense of smell allowed him to recognize and distinguish *maple wood, oakwood, pinewood, elm wood, pearwood, old, young, rotting, moldering, mossy wood, down to single logs, chips, and splinters.* (Süskind, p. 25.)

Another of his quite unusual capacities was the gift to experience an object that he had been observing and smelling (which was even more important!) in a physical way, to the point of becoming one with it. By the way, such a phenomenon was described by schizophrenics who reported experiencing the meaning of particular words as material invasion on their bodies (Wrobel, p.107) — Grenouille *vomited the word up, as if he were filled with wood to his ears, as if buried in wood to his neck, as if his stomach, his throat, his nose were spilling over with wood.* (Süskind, p. 24.)

The central character of *Perfume*, when being almost adult, finally was able to learn language thanks to his unusual way of experiencing surrounding reality. His vocabulary, which referred to experiences perceived through his extraordinary smell, was much more impressive that one of the typical user of the communicative tool that is language. On the other hand, when it came to abstract terms, especially concepts dealing with morality, he remained totally impaired. Anything that could not be perceived by his senses, was foreign to Grenouille.

Much of Süskind's talent as a writer is based on his ability to go beyond boundaries imposed by the common logic that reflects the limits of our language.

As the German author proves, the creative user of our formalized language can apply its binary instruments to a multi-dimensional description. But ironically, this masterful piece of literature significantly challenges the usefulness of language in the interpretation of nature.

The Idols of Francis Bacon

It is not the goal here to discuss human limits of knowledge of the surrounding world, and a serious attempt is made to avoid it. What cannot be evaded is the role of language in the interpretation of reality.

One of the most pondering investigators in this matter was Baron Francis Bacon. In his aphorisms, collected under the title *The New Organon*, he points out the features of our minds that considerably limit proper understanding of reality. He calls them idols and says that their role is to bring us false notions of what we perceive. There are four such false notions: *Idols of the Tribe, Idols of the Cave, Idols of the Market Place and Idols of the Theater.*

Idols of the Tribe deal with the nature of the human race which is not able to catch the true character of reality because of "a false assertion that the sense of man is the measure of things" (an assertion that Bacon explicitly rejects).

The second obstacle to proper understanding, *Idols of the Cave*, is the burden of the knowledge of an individual that is enriched by the influence of authorities that one admires and follows. They cause our minds to be "preoccupied and predisposed," thus not able to interpret on unbiased bases.

The restrictions imposed by *the Idols of the Market Place* come from our contacts with others, and here language clearly plays a prominent role as well: first, "the ill and unfit choices of words wonderfully obstruct the understanding" and then "words plainly force and overrule the understanding, and throw all into confusion, and lead men away into numberless empty controversies and idle fancies."

In fact, the formulation of such an extreme statement should be followed by Bacon's decision to cease writing in order to avoid "numberless empty controversies." Because Bacon did not do it, we must proclaim our reservation toward such a radical opinion.

The fourth cause for our poor understanding of reality comes from the *Idols of the Theater*. What is meant here are "creations" (rules and laws) of science and philosophy presented to us in "an unreal and scenic fashion."

Regarding the heritage of science and its systematic view of the world, Bacon points out an important feature of our linguistic understanding of reality. This scientific presentation of nature is another "gift" that we have received with and from language. Language reflects the systemic way of perception that comes from the classifiable approach presented by science and its methodology. But as a reflection of the world, language is not a passive tool. It has its own aggressive logic that is being imposed on us, the users of language. For instance, from a systemic viewpoint, a sympathetic dolphin is a representative of an aquatic mammal, fishlike in form.

Well (to continue investigating the reasoning and perspective of Bacon), for me, it is not only "fishlike in form" but is simply a fish, and not only because it looks like a fish, but also because it lives in the water. Of course, if my daughter would ask me about the species to which dolphins belong, I would say to her that they are mammals. But deep in my heart, they will remain fish.

Classifications, in any case, allow us to perceive reality according to certain logical orders. Because we share these orders with other users of language, we are able to refer to similar ideas and consequently, to communicate.

Language is an active factor in our contacts with reality and its interpretation. Sometimes it helps us to grasp a complicated process in the form of a handsome aphorism; sometimes it acts as a "mis-shaper" leading us to the peripheries of comprehension; yet at other times it acts as creator of nonexistent realms.

Language, this fantastic, creative artist, presents to us, as the German linguist Johann L. Weisgerber noticed, for example, the Orion constellation and we are thus able to recognize its pattern in the clear night sky.

But what in fact actually exists is an immeasurable collection of stars without this super-imposed order, whose organization we see thanks to the concept of a constellation. Thus, we can see what does not necessarily exist in the way we believe. On the other hand, we often overlook what does exist, if is not important within our hierarchy of linguistic significance.

Another example, also taken from Weisgerber, refers to the world of plants. In our conceptual world, there is no place for weeds. These plants, let us agree, because of their "debased" character, are not included in the human concept of flora.

The World and the Personal World

We live in the world of images, not occurrences. Either we anticipate, interpret, wander through memories, or we are actually experiencing. What is common for all these states is the constant active involvement of our conceptual world. Language serves as an intermediary with significant consequences for us in relation to the external world and us, and in relation to our internal worlds of memories, hopes, and dreams.

Concepts are based on common denominators of human experiences, but in particular cases, they are of course quite individual. My former student who used to live in metropolitan Detroit once spent a wonderful weekend in San Francisco. He happened to be on a yacht, the weather was magnificent, the Golden Gate bridge splendid, the company and cocktails were elegant. Everything on the Bay was in purest contrast to the way his student life had looked in Detroit. That day he made up his mind: the decision was that he would live in San Francisco after he finished his studies. What he planned, he did. When five years after his departure from Detroit, I visited him in San Francisco, he confessed that since settling in the city, he had not yet taken the opportunity to spend a single hour on the bay, not even in a canoe. Still, the two-day-long experience of him on the Bay (not visited by him since then) had been transformed into the significant image that had decided his postgraduate fate. The ways in which we perceive the world, analyze it, understand and fear it—all of them come from our imagination—our own drawings and ideas of reality.

There is a story of a man who wanted to borrow a snow shovel from his neighbor. Going to the neighbor's house the man was talking to himself: "Whomever you approach, that person turns out to be a greedy, selfish pig. People are not generous anymore. I do not believe that this fellow will allow me to use his shovel. No, no, he is not this type of a guy who would lend you a shovel. God! Why people are so selfish? Why me, why did *I* have to get such a bastard for a neighbor..." Meantime he approached the neighbor's door. A fellow from across the street opened the door, greeted the guest and asked him what he could do for him. "Keep your damn snow shovel to yourself!" yelled the visitor, turned around and left deeply angered by the selfishness of others.

Oh yes, the story of the angered man is funny and makes us laugh. But after a while, we may come to the conclusion that this story is more typical than we thought in the first moment. And we may ask ourselves the following question: How many times in our lives have we acted according to such images and feelings about reality, rather than in accordance with facts?

The Very Personal World and the World

Our life is a constant exchange. In addition to exchange with other persons, we communicate with the surrounding world, and with Nature. We have interchanges even with our inner world, being involved in discourse with ourselves. Our exchange with the external world is shaped by our inner engines. When we are happy, the speed of the dialogue is faster and the colors of its background are bright; when our mood is bad, the speed of discourse becomes slow and the colors turn gray. Rarely we realize the intimacy of our perception of the world (so-called objective reality). Speaking plainly, how subjective is our perception of this "objective" surrounding? Filled with a certain mixture of anticipations (hopes), self-images (delusions), and interpretations based on disappointing earlier experiences (disillusions), we start to look at the world with an intimate prejudice. Of course, we are not often aware of the existence of our extreme bias; rarely we admit to ourselves that what we call "perception" is rather "projection." Actually, when we start considering some situation, what we are really attempting to do is to recreate the world according to our anticipation. Each time we recreate it, we do so in accordance with to the contents of the mixture of ingredients that have just been discussed.

The situation becomes even more complicated when another person is involved. From the point of view of a sender, the art of communication involves at least two dimensions: the content and the wrapping, or what we want to say and the way we want to say it. Nevertheless, further realization of the communicative goals we intended does not depend on us; since the moment we articulate our messages, they obtain their own, independent beings, and rely on the receiver's intentions regarding interpretation. Usually the receiver cooperates with us in the process of communication. Usually, but not always, as in this story told by Milan Kundera:

> *Once upon a time, in the early part of the century, there lived a poet. He was so old he had to be taken on walks by his amanuensis. "Master," his amanuensis said one day, "look what's up in the sky! It's the first airplane ever to fly over the city!" "I have my own picture of it," said the poet to his amanuensis, without raising his eyes from the ground.*
> M. Kundera, *The Unbearable Lightness of Being*,
> 1987, p. 82.

The poet's attitude reminds us of a cartoon by T. Thaves in which a customer in an eyeglass store states: "They don't have to be expansive... I already know what most things looks like."

A substantial part of our activities is devoted to interpretations of so-called objective reality. We spend endless hours guessing the meaning of events we consider important; on the other hand, we waste no time reading into insignificant happenings.

Later we may determine that we wasted our time investing in the interpretation of meaningless episodes while leaving the important occurrences unattended. The task is immense indeed; what we try to do is to decipher accurately what sometimes remains unrevealed even to the author of a message. This is considering and bringing attention to those rare situations when we are saying something not knowing what and why, when we are not sure of our own intentions.

Let us consider "The End of the World" by Skeeter Davies, a once-popular song that well reflects the interdependence of what actually happens and what we think about it, where we can sense the supremacy of the personal world over the "objective" reality. The lyrics starts with a woman being surprise that the sun is shining and the sea moves its waves and poses the question:

> Don't they know it's the end of the world
> 'cause you don't love me anymore.

There is the end of the love, so why is it that the birds continue to sing, stars continue to shine, and the entire world goes on, rather than ceasing to exist?

One could argue that the best description of this song's lyrics is that they are banal. But the lyrics' platitudes could hardly be surpassed by philosophical writings in these apt descriptions of the impact of our emotional experience on our perception of the so-called objective world. Do you remember the day when you found out that a beloved person shared the same affection towards you? Do you recall the highly appreciated lightness of being of that day, or its physical dimension: what you were carrying was just less heavy, the sun seemed to shine brighter or maybe cloudiness and even wet snow looked less unbearable for you.

Again, let us turn to another song titled "This Is My Song" (written by Charlie Chaplin, performed by Petula Clark). In this song, one reports on her happiness, the lightness of her heart, the brightness of the stars, and the beautiful color of the sky. She also states:

Contact 17

Flowers are smiling bright (...)
For the world: you and me...

Yes, you have noticed: *For the world: you and me*—in this song, the meaning of the term "world" is *you and me*, which means that the rest of humankind may well just not exist.

The "world" as understood here is a subjective world. And being quite serious now, the description declaring that *flowers are smiling brightly* seems to be quite correct in context. It is an entirely other question if this description is objective. With flowers, it is not easy matter to decide. Would it be less subjective to propose *flowers are crying shrilly*? This should be left to the reader's consideration.

SECOND LONGING:
CONTACT WITH OTHERS

A Soft Tongue Breaketh the Bone

Imagine two people talking about dolphins. One associates those beings with mammals, another with fish. Are they talking about dolphins or rather about images or concepts of them? Or, let us listen to the following exchange: A asks B, "What do you call somebody who killed his mother and father?" B answers, "An orphan." Communication in those examples is not about reality, but about its representations. It happens this way because while communicating we are constantly using filters of images which delimit our perception of reality.

Hope drives us when we speak. We look forward to expressing ourselves and shaping surrounding reality. When we talk, we believe in achieving at least the first of two main aims: that we will be understood, and that we will be able to convince our interlocutor to act in the way we suggest. The first goal is more spiritual or mental, the second is more practical. Accomplishment of the latter depends on our skills in terms of suggestion, and on the susceptibility of the other person to our eloquence. Realization of the former, especially when a message goes beyond the routine of everyday conversation and involves more personal contents of psychological character, depends on the degree of soulmateness with a communicative partner. Fulfillment of this goal can lead to establishing or deepening of contact between such persons who may then recognize themselves as kindred spirits.

The first aim of the act of speaking fulfills the communicative function, the second one — the pragmatic one. Consequently, in terms of verbal communication, the theory of language distinguishes the two abilities of the speaker: the ability to express oneself verbally, which is called linguistic competence; and the capacity to choose the best linguistic tools in particular communicative situations we speak of as pragmatic competence. Of course, in conversation, in addition to speaking, we also listen, and while listening, we constantly adjust the two aspects of the verbal performance: what we want to say, and the way in which our message is to be said. But spoken communication is not a sequence of consecutive monologues of speaker A and speaker B—it is rather an active dialogue between the interlocutors. Therefore, a skillful communicator is not only a capable sender; such a person is, simultaneously, a competent receiver of the message. Relatedly, Colossians 4:6 included the following advice for users of language: *Let your speech be always with grace, seasoned with salt* [that is, with wisdom], *that ye may know how ye ought to answer every man.*

Though linguistic pragmatics was developed as an independent field in language theory only in the twentieth century, the awareness of the importance of pragmatic competence may be traced back to the ancients. As already mentioned, the most common goal of one who undertakes the effort of speaking is to be understood, and the interlocutor's proper comprehension is often only a prelude to the desired action that is transmitted to the listener by the speaker. The quotation for this chapter, from Proverbs 25:15, *a soft tongue breaketh the bone*, refers to the art of patiently and consequently persuading someone peacefully to our viewpoint.

Speech is one of the most important and effective tools we have in terms of influencing the behavior of the others. We suggest, persuade, convince, ask, order, force, blackmail, etc., using words; no wonder that another line from Proverbs 25:11 says: *A word fitly spoken is like apples of gold in settings of silver.* Simultaneously, we ourselves are the constant subjects of suggestions, persuasions, orders, etc. that come from others. Communication is an exchange, and our interlocutors may also own "the apples of gold." Here conflict of interests between the persons participating in conversation usually appears. When A and B have contradictory goals, communication is transformed into confrontation and persuasive abilities become very important.

The art of leading a dispute in which the aim is not achieving the truth, but rather a desired pragmatic goal, is called *eristic*. The Sophists, philosophers of Ancient Greece, were the most famous users and teachers of linguistic manipulation. When we complain about today's language of propaganda, negative campaigns before elections, the populism of politicians, dishonesty and the manipulative use of language of advertisement, and the abuse of language for the sake of moral relativism, we should have in our minds that five centuries BCE, the Sophists had been selling counseling services and teaching linguistic pragmatics. One of the skills that were taught by them was the art of effective lying.

Contemporary linguistic pragmatics focuses on the most effective ways of using language to achieve a specific goal. According to modern pragmatic standards in linguistics, to be competent communicatively means not only to be able to say something, but also to be able to choose the best linguistic means, taking into account the point of view of the interlocutor, the situation, and the purposes one wishes to achieve. When the speaker or writer obtains the gains sought, we call such communication a successful one (on this practical level of considerations).

Although speech is the most effective communicative tool, communicative silence may be as powerful. Two semantic extremes come to mind in this case—either the most negative communication, when we refuse to participate in informative exchange, or the most advanced one, between people who understand each other so well that a limited number (if any) of words is needed to obtain full and deep comprehension.

Understanding, or, When I Mean What You Think I Mean

The term *to understand* means first of all *to recognize a meaning* or, in a broader sense, *to decode a message*. Among the other meanings of *to understand,* the most common one seems to be the one that refers to *the mental ability of comprehension of a particular knowledge.*

The expression *to understand* is a combination of two words: *under* and *stand*. The Anglo-Saxon *under* had two meanings: *beneath* and *among*. The former one is more frequent, but our attention is directed toward the latter one: *to understand* means to us *to be among those who stand*. The part *stand* is cognate with the Sanskrit *sthā: to stand*. Those "who stand" are people who were initiated into a shared comprehension. Simply speaking, *to understand* means *to be among those who are able to comprehend.* Being *among* is *to be a part of a group; to have closer ties with those who belong, than those who do not belong; to share a kind of spiritual brotherhood.*

The phrase *to recognize a meaning* may be expressed in many ways. Let us take a look at its stylistic and semantic richness.

The attempt is to comprehend what a person means, when saying: "I understand." The variety of verbalizations observable in this case refers to formal and informal manners of expressions, to literal and figurative enunciations, and to emotionally meaningful statements. The variety here indicates the importance and sophistication of the concept *to understand*—this crucial semantic ingredient of our core idea: **contact through exchange**.

At the formal level, we deal with such terms as *comprehend, apprehend,* or *perceive the meaning*. The less formal expressions appeal to the figurative sense. A meaning becomes "materialized," allowing the users of the language to *catch, follow, get, grasp, see,* or *seize* it. But there is a degree of comprehension that goes beyond "grasping" a meaning. *To understand completely* means to be able to *be with someone, get into* or even *through one's head, read someone loud and clear,* sometimes *like a book,* and *see to the bottom* even *with half an eye.* On the other hand, there are those who fail to confront the messages, which remain impenetrable for them. Such a *message escapes them, they are lost, at sea, out of their depth, unable to account for it, unable to get it into their head (thick skull),* and *unable to see.*

The one who *does understand* may also be involved in a given instance in a communion of *understanding*. The most significant difference between those terms is that the verbal expression *to understand* refers to the comprehension of the person who received a message. The noun *understanding* alludes to an accord of at least two participants of a communicative act. Those happy persons who are connected by the ties of a reciprocal affection of intellects, enjoy *bonds of harmony, good karma,* and *vibrations, like-mindedness, a meeting of minds, oneness,* and *togetherness.*

An ability to understand the other may be a first step toward relationship. Like-mindedness supported by a similar sensitivity sometimes grows into friendship, sometimes sparks love. Those blessed with the existence of an understanding other, can more easily survive in a communicative bazaar—with its loudness, pragmatism, triteness, simplifications, artificiality, and vulgarity. The spiritual fellowship brought on by the oneness of minds stimulates strength: that is why together we can build Babylon or take it apart. As my friend put it, "What I miss most, is having an understanding other. Sometimes I feel so sad that there is no one with whom to share my innermost thoughts. Writing them in a diary is not the same as holding them up for examination or dissecting them with an understanding person."

Lack of Understanding, or, Superiority of Common Speech

Language is a system that operates according to a limited number of rules. Thanks to those grammatical patterns, we may use words, change their meanings by putting them together, and connect them into sentences. Clarity of linguistic guidelines allows usage of language regardless of the level of education, and does not require an extraordinary intelligence or memory. Of course, when it comes to the poetic description of spring, a very proficient user of language who also has artistic talent is needed. Fortunately, basic communication does not require talent because it is simple. But linguistic simplicity is a mixed blessing. We are lucky in everyday situations—the commonness of the language is compatible with its triviality. We are nevertheless in trouble when we face to the extraordinary. It is not only that the linguistic tool is imperfect; its users are, in addition, usually not ready to go beyond typical, hackneyed communicative settings. The problem is the listeners' indifference to substantial, personal matters. An unwillingness of an interlocutor to listen to really important themes often comes from the fact that those themes are frequently disturbing. As Albert Camus pointed out in *The Plague*, talking about feelings usually led to significant frustration if not to painful disappointment. What was coming out of passion and the depth of sorrow was interpreted in the most conventional, trivial way; the dreadful banknote of drama was exchanged for petty and shallow coins of everyday small-talk:

> *Only on these terms could the prisoners of the plague ensure the sympathy of their concierge and the interest of their hearers.*
> (Albert Camus, *The Plague* (p. 76).

The inhabitants of the plagued Oran had gone through extraordinary experiences but they did not have a real chance to talk about them. The most crucial and painful event which has been affecting their lives, had to remain excluded from conversations. Those who wanted to communicate had to accept the non-written rule of omitting a taboo topic despite the fact that "it" directed and organized life for the Oranians at that time: you simply don't talk about a rope in the home of the hanged man. The common, clichéd language had to be used if communication was to occur at all.

One of the reasons that it is so difficult to find a reciprocal listener comes from indifference. People's preoccupation with their own problems does not incline them to openness toward the other's troubled life. It is true that tragedies, either general, like floods or earthquakes or personal, as a fire or kidnapping, motivate common reactions full of understanding and compassion. But on the less spectacular level of serious and dramatic personal hardships, the emotional tortures of other people mostly go unnoticed by us. This is why people connect themselves to groups organized according to their special problems. AA (Alcoholics Anonymous) members, families of those touched by Alzheimer's disease, mothers of children suffering from leukemia, and other associations offer what cannot be found among those who are free from such problems. Sharing and understanding of mutually experienced suffering is a main criterion of belonging and the biggest award for those who join such groups.

The preciousness and uniqueness of a real experience of contact is not always being understood, but the presence of somebody with whom one may share a significant experience is typically quite intensely appreciated.

As Ted Hawkins put it in his discussion of his blues song "The Good and the Bad," life may be good when there is somebody to be with; laughter may be not good when it is shared with no one, dying may be good when we are not loved anymore, and

> Talking is bad
> If you've got no one to talk to.

Misunderstanding One Another, or, What I (incorrectly) Think You Think vs. What You (incorrectly) Think I Think

An act of communication, when it occurs, is the culmination of a complicated, multidimensional process of uncountable conscious and unconscious preparations. The very moment when the communicative exchange takes a verbal form may be compared to the act of signing a treaty by the presidents of two governments. We are well aware that before signatures are put on paper, a lengthy and uneasy procedure of preparations takes place. It usually includes the involvement of dozens of specialists in the field which the treaty refers to, professional negotiators, members of particular state commissions, etc. When we are watching the final ceremony on a TV screen, we see only a modicum of the constituent elements.

Similarly, an act of communication is the resultant encounter that comes from numerous factors: who and what we are, who and what our interlocutor is, and what the circumstances of the event are, among others. Usually, before we start to talk, we make a careful assessment of a given communicative context, which is possible, thanks to our extensive experience. Unfortunately, regardless of the amount of attention we involve in such a process, there is no guarantee of successful comprehension, as illustrated in the following example. A group of friends decides to buy a psychiatric clinic. To conclude the transaction, they visit the place that soon was to be managed by them. Oliveira, the prospective director of the clinic, while wandering through its corridors, was approached by a smiling young man who took his hand and cheerfully swinging their arms led him to the freight elevator. The visitor appreciated idea of having a psychiatric ward tour given by one of the "madman," and treated the guide with cigarette, which was accepted by him with a whistle of joy.

> *Then it turned out that he was an attendant and that Oliveira was not a patient, the usual misunderstandings in cases like that.*
> J. Cortazar, *Hopscotch*, p. 298.

What led Oliveira to the conviction that the young man he had met was a patient? Theoretically, he might meet there either a staff member, a patient, or a visiting family member. The visitors are usually easily recognizable because of the way they act or are dressed. Oliveira had to obtain enough information to eliminate the possibility that the stranger was a visitor. In his next step, he had to decide if the approaching man was a staff member or a patient. Why did Oliveira eliminate the likelihood of facing a doctor or an attendant? Why, conversely, did the attendant believe that Oliveira was a patient? The non-verbal communication cues between the two partners in misunderstanding were interpreted by their respective guesses, which were rooted in their own specific experiences and knowledge: first, Oliveira noticed the man's smile, and one of the common stereotypes of a patient of a psychiatric ward is his childish behavior that may include an "inappropriate" smile. This initial impression was later strengthened by the fact that the man took Oliveira by the hand, and swung his arm. Oliveira responded to these cues characteristically, offering his companion a cigarette, one of the most precious goods in a psychiatric ward. Reacting to this gesture by "whistling with satisfaction," Oliveira's guide misled him further. Of course, the attendant did not intentionally deceive Oliveira—he reacted in the way that, according to his experience with his patients, would please someone in his care.

The comicality of the situation comes from the fact that Oliveira and his guide became victims of their careful efforts, which were to address the particular communicative patterns typical of the psychiatric ward environment. It did not work and both men created the impressions that they were patients themselves. In this way each of them fooled the other, but simultaneously himself, thinking that his partner had thought of him as a sane person.

We may even say that success (or its lack) of prospective communication depends on the distance between self-image and the image formed and kept by others. What others think of us usually takes a quite wishful shape in our own minds. The image we believe our communicative partners have of us is of crucial importance because it pertains to the two main factors in a speech act: who speaks, and to whom. Based on it, we decide which proper communicative tools to choose.

When we communicate directly, we have a good chance of achieving correct comprehension in most cases. The situation becomes more complicated when we consider a metaphoric expression. People who know each other well, develop a personalized version of language, and the uninitiated may not be able to comprehend a message that is coded in this way. Let us say that we are in Geneva and we witness a dialogue of an unidentified couple.

Contact

He asks her if she would like to go to Palermo, and she answers: "I prefer Geneva." The woman's reaction saddens him and we, being deprived of additional information, will be left with our guesses. Knowing both cities, we may (or may not) wonder, why she did not want to go to Palermo, or we can assume that by saying this, she really meant that she did like (or was afraid) to travel.

Our comprehension of this situation will be dramatically changed with new information available:

> *Franz was sad. He had grown so accustomed to linking their love life to foreign travels that his "Let's go to Palermo!" was an unambiguous erotic message and her "I prefer Geneva" could have only one meaning: his mistress no longer desired him.*
> M. Kundera, *The Unbearable Lightness of Being*, p. 82.

The hidden meanings now revealed allow us to understand the secret meaning of language of these lovers. In the light of additional explanations, the very short dialogue we have witnessed suddenly reveals to us the intimate sphere of the life of Sabina and Franz. "He must be a poor lover," some of shrewd observers will presume, "she has another lover" others, gifted with a hunch, will state, unless they discover the true story from the all-knowing narrator, who lets us know that Franz's mistress went to another room, brought a bottle of wine, opened it, and filled two glasses with it. Only then was Franz able to relax, having discovered that

> *The "I prefer Geneva" did not mean she refused to make love; quite the contrary, it meant she was tired of limiting their lovemaking to foreign cities.*
> M. Kundera, *The Unbearable Lightness of Being*, p. 83.

Following Sabina and Franz in their intimate communication we find that even between partners experienced and sophisticated in metaphoric communication as well as in their private linguistic code, the less literal meanings are, the better the chances for misunderstandings, as the following cartoon shows:

Conditions of a Successful Speech Act

Diogenes (or Diogenes Laertios) in his *Lives of Eminent Philosophers* presents Plato's understanding of the correct speech:

> *Successful speaking has four parts. The first consists in speaking to the purpose, the next, to the requisite length, the third, before the proper audience, and the fourth, at the proper moment. What is to the purpose is what is likely to be expedient for speaker and hearer. The requisite length is that which is neither more nor less than enough. To speak to the proper audience means this: in addressing persons older than yourself, the discourse must be made suitable to the audience as being elderly men; whereas in addressing juniors the discourse must be suitable to young men. The proper time of speaking is neither too soon nor too late; otherwise you will miss the mark and not speak with success.*

Plato stressed the four elements of a successful speech: (1) proper subject with regard to a purpose (about what and why), (2) proper length (how long), (3) proper style (how, with regard to whom), and (4) proper time (when). We today I this era of linguistic pragmatics may be struck by the astuteness of his remarks and their application of the elements of Ancient Greek analysis. The only difference is that today additional elements are taken into consideration: (5) proper place (where), and (6) proper distance (from where).

Considering the importance of place, we cannot disregard common habits, (expectations) in this matter: if we want to discuss a theory that focuses on the strong Romanesque influence in a style of city walls of Magliano in Toscana—do not confuse it with the city of Magliano in Sabina, in Latium!—the lobby of a movie theater is not the best place to try to do this.

Concerning the significance of time: should an academic advisor be approached by a student three minutes before her class starts with her idea of changing a major from physics into physical education? And thinking about timing, let us stress again the importance of Plato's advice on proper length of talking: paraphrasing words from Shakespeare's *Richard III,* we might say: "How sour sweet talk is, when time is broke and no proportion kept!" As to the proper physical distance between speaker and listener, the cultural habits of an environment should be followed in order to avoid discomfort on the part of the listener.

The six conditions just briefly discussed, although they offer an apt description of the essentials of good communication, cannot guarantee the achievement of understanding. By fulfilling them, we undoubtedly increase the chance of comprehension. We, however, cannot overcome factors that are beyond our control, and, in fact, beyond anyone's control. If the interlocutor is overwhelmed by serious personal problems, the best possible presentation will not make an effective case for the speaker. And what about the possibility, as irrational as it may be, that the person spoken to in the most effective manner, simply does not like the speaker? Conversely, when the speaker is liked: how easy the possible obstacles created by imperfect eloquence are overcome!

Finally, another element should be mentioned. No matter how exactly we operate according to the prescription for successful speech, the goal will not be achieved if we fail to fulfill the requirement of credibility. The most obvious examples might be taken from the territory of lies, though falsifying or fabricating does not necessarily lead to a communicative fiasco. As the lesson from *The Berenstain Bears and the Truth* (p. 1) states: *No matter how you hope, no matter how you try, you can't make truth, out of a lie.*

On the other hand, even when the truth is told, a message may simply not fit a hearer's expectations (prejudices), a common misfortune of ill-fated originators who were not able to overcome the disbelief of would-be receivers of their proposals. If the message does not fit the expectations of the receiver, even the most powerful content of truth will not be appealing. Let us consider the Watergate scandal and the Soviet Union propaganda machine that ignored this event and did not use it in order to discredit American system. The problem was that the Watergate scandal might impress only the receivers in democratic settings: the government broke in to the hotel room and bugged it... *So?*, as Yakov Smirnoff (1993) put it: *In Russia we call it a room service!*

Mismanaged lies are behind the most notorious cases of failure in achieving a communicative goal. Lack of credibility, which might be called the Rabbit's Syndrome (see quotation below), leads to an unsuccessful information exchange because one participant's account does not match another's linguistic and epistemological understanding, as in the following example:

> *"Is anybody at home?"*
> *There was a sudden scuffling noise from inside the hole, and then silence.*
> *"What I said was, 'Is anybody at home?'" called out Pooh very loudly.*
> *"No!" said a voice; and then added, "you needn't shout so loud. I heard you quite well the first time."*
> *"Bother!" said Pooh. "Isn't there anybody here at all?"*
> *"Nobody."*
> *Winnie-the-Pooh took his head out of the hole, and thought for a little, and he thought to himself, "There must be somebody there, because somebody must have said 'Nobody.'" So he put his head back in the hole, and said:*
> *"Hallo, Rabbit, isn't that you?"*
> *"No," said Rabbit, in a different sort of voice this time.*
>
> A. A. Milne, *Winnie-The-Pooh*, pp. 22-23.

What Does the Human Face Communicate?

There are stories that once heard can stay in your memory forever. One that still occupies my mind is an account by a friend who suffers from epilepsy. According to him, every time he is brought back to the realm of awareness after severe attacks, the first image that he sees invariably astonishes him with its beauty. Fortunately, in a critical moment, there has always been somebody around to help him. In this way his awakenings and returns to reality were connected with the presence and view of the other human being. In his words, regardless whose face he sees in such moments, the impression he gets is always the same: there is nothing more beautiful under the sun than a human face.

The face, the most distinguishable and unique part of the human body, fascinates and inspires, seduces and horrifies, generates the most sublime admiration of painters and poets, and is the most important non-verbal element of communication and contact. It is true that the physical presence of our interlocutor is not a necessary condition for communication to occur; an announcement by the voice recorder of an answering machine, a letter, or a message on a computer screen would be enough. However, when a participant of the communicative act strives for contact, the physical existence of another is very desirable. Even when we talk to somebody in our minds, in many cases an image of that person accompanies our speechless conversation.

The human face, the mystical culmination of our physical appearance, astonishes with its complexity and completeness. For man, who is sometimes described as a microcosm, his face creates a micro-universe by itself. William Blake described the four substances of its composition in the following way: *the eyes of fire, the nostrils of air, the mouth of water, the beard of earth*. Among the four elements, eyes always attract the most interest and descriptions.

Both the face and eyes are commonly perceived as very important communicative tools; the true and meaningful conversation is the *face-to-face* one with *direct eye-contact* as a must. But if eyes are treated as a trustful source of knowledge about the true intentions of an interlocutor, a face—with respect to such insight—does not enjoy a good reputation. Common understanding of the relationship between the face and heart or soul (the attributes of truth) and between them and eyes, is aptly illustrated by proverbs: *The eyes are the window of the soul; the understanding of an Arab is in his eyes; the heart's letter is read in the eyes; in the forehead and the eye, the lecture of the mind doth lie*. But, on the other hand, listen to following sayings: *The face is no index to the heart*, and *fair face, foul heart*. What the face tries to hide, the eyes reveal—this seems to be the message.

The eyes of the other, those powerful communicators, are helpful guides into the realm of the interlocutor's feelings, but may turn into enemies, piercing like swords. As Ralph Waldo Emerson, an unquestionable expert in the eyes' power, noticed: *An eye can threaten like a loaded and leveled gun, or it can insult like hissing or kicking; or, in its altered mood, by beams of kindness, it can make the heart dance for joy.* Comparing the effectiveness of language with the subtlety and charm of the eye's talk, the same author wrote: *One of the most wonderful things in nature is a glance of the eye; it transcends speech; it is the bodily symbol of identity.*

The two communicative extremes to which the eyes go, from a tender glimpse to an executing glare, properly reflect the two ultimate meanings of silence: when we refuse to talk because we hate, and when we are still because we do not need words to understand each other fully.

Let us turn now a writer who seems to solve the mystery of establishing and maintaining contact, the key concept in our discussion of understanding. This is the way in which Antoine de Saint-Exupéry described the birth of contact between two lonely souls— the little prince and the fox, in *The Little Prince*. The unhappy Little Prince invites the fox to play with him. The animal refuses on the grounds of not being tamed. The boy does not understand the concept of taming, so the fox explains that to tame means to establish ties with somebody:

> *"To me, you are still nothing more than a little boy who is just like hundred thousand other little boys. And I have no need of you. To you, I am nothing more than a fox like as hundred thousand other foxes. But if you tame me, than we shall need each other. To me, you will be unique in all the world. To you, I shall be unique in all the world..."*
>
> Antoine de Saint-Exupéry, *Le Petit Prince*, 1943, p. 78.

Later, the fox complains about his life, which is boring and uneventful: either he hunts chicken or he is the object of hunting. Everything in his life is predictable, there is no novelty and nothing to wait for. It could be dramatically changed by the act of taming: there will be no more boring days: suddenly, the sound of steps of one, unique person in the world, the very special one, will bring joy and purpose to the fox's life. Also, the common golden color of the wheat fields will gain a distinguished character because it will trigger the associations with the tint of the boy's hair. The wheat that had had no meaning for the fox will become something desired and important.

> "What must I do, to tame you?" asked the little prince. "You must be very patient," replied the fox. "First you will sit down at a little distance from me—like that—in the grass. I shall look at you out of the corner of my eye, and you will say nothing. Words are the source of misunderstandings. But you will sit a little closer to me, every day..."
> Antoine de Saint-Exupéry, *Le Petit Prince*, 1943, p. 84.

To establish contact and maintain it: these two belong to the most fulfilling and rewarding emotional achievements of a human being. Why? Because there is nothing more fascinating, rewarding, and inspiring than to find somebody who understands you and whom you understand.

A Word on Electronic Communication

Recent decades brought a true revolution in communication. Popularity and commonness of paging systems that can reach you anywhere at anytime, cellular phones allowing you to make or receive a phone call in a car or during hiking; widespread e-mail connecting users among themselves and with almost the entire world in seconds, tweeting, and facebooking—what does it mean?

The last phenomenon, especially, attracts some people so intensively that according to their accounts, they spend up to eighteen hours per day in front of a computer screen, communicating with dozens of other addicted users of personal computers. Does this perhaps reflect American difficulties with face-to-face communication? Maybe it is just easier to exchange information within a virtual-type discussion group than to face a partner.

There are signs that many e-mail users are strongly attracted by the anonymity that it allows. Namelessness or the use of pseudonyms allows the user either to be wrapped in clouds or to wear a mask. In this way, two among the three crucial elements of the communicative process, a sender (A) and a receiver (B), can disguise themselves, eliminating the steadfast platform of conversational references those features otherwise provide.

It is not uncommon among the users of popular computer networks to present themselves as somebody else. For example Ms. A pretends that she is a man, and her/his computer mate, Mrs. B makes Ms./Mr. A believe that she is a high-school junior. In this way both communicators put themselves into a mode where neither participant takes real responsibility for a message that is sent.

Faceless and eyeless others offer unimaginable chances for exchange of information, but award no opportunity for contact. Looking at computer/telephone screens, "talking" to virtual electronic partners, texting or tweeting them, taking an ephemeral break only to listen to a voice mail and to read a routine, incoming fax, slowly but surely, we may transform ourselves into communicative robots.

THIRD LONGING:
CONTACT BETWEEN HER AND HIM

A Beautiful Angel of Death

One of the finest Polish poets of the twentieth century, Jan Lechoń (Leszek Józef Serafinowicz, 1899-1956), gave the following description of the two most important things in human life:

You ask: what in all of my life is most vital
I'll answer: Death and Love, these two are quite equal,
I fear the one's black eyes, fear the blue ones no less,
Each of these is my love, and they both are my deaths.

Through the blackest of nights, through the heavens all
    starry,
These two impel the great wind interplanetary,
Which so blew once, Earth yielded up Man in that night,
For eternal soul's sorrow, and body's delight.

We grind the days to granules, plumb life to the depths,
Deepest truths of existence to dig out and gauge,
And know this one thing only: that nothing does change,
Death protects us from love, as love shields us from death.
Jan Lechoń , Pytasz, co w moim życiu
z wszystkich rzeczą główną,
Translated by Marcel Weyland.

An art school graduate told me the story of a professor who was not popular among the students because he was not a talented teacher; nevertheless, he intrigued her because of his unusual talent and achievements in his artistic field. When the time arrived to take advanced courses, she decided to choose him to be her mentor in directed studies.

As soon as they met for the first session she found that the professor, unorganized as usual, did not have a detailed plan for her assignment, but shared with her what he believed was the only occupation worthy of the human mind and talent: solving the mystery of love and death.

The connection between these two phenomena was aptly described by Thornton Wilder, who wrote: *there is a land of the living and a land of the dead and the bridge is love, the only survival, the only meaning.*

Those who have loved have a number of stories that speak to us of Wilder's "bridge" of love and of its linking the living and the dead: in dealing with contacts with the Invisible World, the closeness between Eros, the god of love, and Thanatos, the god of death, becomes obvious. But there is one more phenomenon involved here: time. In a discussion of the wonder of love, time cannot be omitted, and in a discussion of time, associations with death are inescapable.

Common in the Western iconographic personification of death is a portrayal of him as a skeleton with a scythe.

An interesting exception to this tendency can be found in paintings of Jacek Malczewski, the Polish twentieth century artist, who pictured death as a half-clothed, beautiful and sensual girl holding a scythe who closes the eyes of an old man, preparing him for his last sleep.

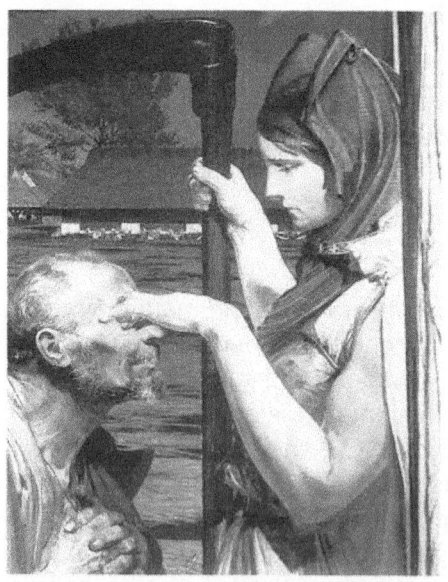

The loving touch or even seductiveness (as expressed by Malczewski) of death, who brings ultimate relief, reflects an eternal ambiguity surrounding *the sleeping partner of our life*, as Horace Smith called her, so brilliantly articulated by Shakespeare in Hamlet's famous monologue:

> *To be, or not to be: that is the question:*
> *Whether 'tis nobler in the mind to suffer*
> *The slings and arrows of outrageous fortune,*
> *Or to take arms against a sea of troubles,*
> *And by opposing end them? To die: to sleep...*

Love can give us a sense of staying among the living; love can rescue someone who has established ties with death; and tragic love may burn out the life force and lead to the embrace of the pale rider, death. Tristan and Isold, Cleopatra and Mark Anthony, and Romeo and Juliet, all found a shelter for their love in death. In this way, their passion was immortalized.

Ecstasy is not a terrestrial experience. Lovers who take a cosmic journey enter timeless celestial fields cultivated by Memory and her sister Death. In the bright and silent passageway the lovers pass travelers who are alone; the one-way sleepwalkers.

Time and the Landscape of Memory

Joost A.M. Meerloo in his essay "The Time Sense in Psychiatry" indicates an important difference between man who is capable of living not only in the present, but also in the past and in the future, and animals that are believed to live only in the present moment. Another distinguishing feature of the human being or "communicating animal" is his/her capacity to turn biological signs of either pleasure or dissatisfaction into symbolic entities:

> *Man's highest expressive deed, the word, has become a polyphonous sign, an ambassador of his instinctual archaic needs. Through speech and words man learns to handle symbols and to condense reality into simple verbal signs. Man captures time and duration through his creative acts, his rhythms, words and cadences, his mathematical figures, poems and historical dreams. Thus the symbol as a historical*

communication became the inherited psychological gene and time-binding messenger of ancient traditional concepts.
Joost A. M. Meerloo,
in Fraser, J. T., ed., *The Voices of Time*, p. 240.

According to Meerloo, man is able to "condense" reality into a symbol. One word names something that could have existed for centuries—in this way we condense not only concepts, but also time. This ability of compressing time is characteristic of highly intense, emotional experiences. One among such emotions is love.

Time is indissolubly connected with the intimacy of experiences, fulfillments, and confessions. Our sense of time depends on the intensity of experiencing it. With an increase in its dynamism, it grows substantiality. The denser the time, the longer and deeper it is imprinted in memory. The importance of contacts, in addition to their lengths, which are reflected in "horizontal" memory, should also be measured according to their depth, which is scored in the "vertical" dimension of human memory. There are contacts that for external observers appear no longer than a blink of an eye, to them are almost unnoticed, and in the chronicle written by the hand of such observers are not recorded. Those very same contacts, because of their depths, can have an epochal meaning for those who have experienced them. *Those two minutes in which I really lived!* said Fyodor Dostoyevsky commenting on the intensity of his experience.

Known first of all for its ability to condense time in the highest degree, hence from its presence in the vertical sense of memory, love has the prerogative to mark both dimensions of our memory deeply. Because of its magic, love simultaneously captures all senses, preventing its possessor from noticing little but this feeling. The time of those deeply in love is mainly vertical. The deeper the contact between the two, the deeper they enter into the tunnel of time. In linear time, perceived according to calendar order, time is experienced as open, as endless. In the realm of time that is experienced in love, which one enters more deeply, flexibility does not exist, and intensity is measured by the level of density.

When we investigate the weight of past occurrences, we should call as witnesses those segments of memory that are filled to the highest degree. In the linear landscape of the valley of memory those segments create mountains, sometimes even an entire mountain range. There are separate segments filled with just the single armchair, the leaf, the song, the bus, the sandy beach, the smile, the telephone conversation, the square, and certain hugs much fuller than volumes of romances. It is so, because there are people and their matters that exist in memory against time. The density of such experiences creates a landscape of memory, mainly marked by its vertical dimension that cannot be balanced by logic, which exists in the horizontal order, no matter how many witnesses logic could bring to testify against the vertical landscape of love.

And what of the woman and man of this chapter, and the contact between them? They are enriched because they met, and then they could say with Dostoyevsky that they really lived.

The Ultimate Exchange

There is nothing more intense, inspiring, mystical, and more magical than to meet another human being who understands you and whom you understand. When in addition to this fascination, this intellectual magic—the magic of body, the erotic fascination also appears—then what happens?

We can say that there is nothing more intense, both exciting and painful, inspiring and devastating, more mystical and magical, than to meet another human being who understands you and whom you understand, and to fall in love.

> *I hold it true, whate'er befall;*
> *I feel it, when I sorrow most;*
> *'Tis better to have loved and lost*
> *Than never to have loved at all.*

Not without passionate reason did Alfred Lord Tennyson write these well-known lines.

Love reorganizes our communicative system. It brings a special light to silent, darkened areas, and simultaneously blinds other territories through the intensity of its brightness. Those territories are responsible for rational, sober calculation, the ability to foresee, and the weaving together of experiences; they also provide us with defensive strategies. Taken from these territories, we become disarmed and unprotected against the one with whom we fall in love.

The military terminology used here is adequate, nevertheless, from the point of view of a person in love; this defenseless condition is desirable. "Sweet bondage" is self-imposed and expresses absolute acceptance of another person. Touch, kiss, erotica—they lead to the ultimate exchange in which you give yourself, and simultaneously accept another person to the extent of amalgamating The Two into One.

True love is freed from the constraints of selfishness and is based on the desire for giving, not on the passion for possessing. Metaphysical fulfillment, the paranormal exchange, can occur only in erotica that is rooted in a desire for giving.

On the other hand, "to possess somebody," means to become a one-way communicator. In such communication the selfish partner uses the other as a mirror that reflects alleged perfection of the one portrayed. An egoist becomes involved in romance and even marriage out of self-satisfaction. The information that yells out here speaks of the possessor's attractiveness, or intelligence, or abilities in the domain of interpersonal conquest, or perhaps of something else, but always is clearly intended to add positive elements to the self-image of the sender of such a presentation of a personal attitude.

In such situation the other person is subjected. One-way communication takes place and there is no trace of partnership. It does not mean that every person who looks for affirmation of his values in relationship is selfish. In our contacts we long for acceptance from our partner, but we also understand that our mate looks for the same. So we exchange such feelings, bringing ourselves closer to each other. If the ideal is *an exchange*, then the one-way communication we have described must be considered as a failing one. This pseudo-communication is humiliating to the subjected partner.

The noun "possessor" is commonly associated with man and this association reflects male-dominated relationships. A man of the macho-type, a lady-killer, a conqueror, a heart-breaker, a Don Juan, is considered here in a better version; in the worst scenario, he would be a rapist, a wife-beater, an intimidating and humiliating sexual harasser, etc.

It would be unjust, however, to deprive women of the power which they can perfectly exercise, if they so desire. The international term appropriate here is a *femme fatale*, a sure troublemaker for man.

Leonard Cohen describes one of them in his song "Light as the Breeze," in his 1992 album, *The Future*. The obviously beautiful, naked lady who is dancing in a graceful way plays a game with her man. She teases him, but at the same time allows him to worship her, "as long as you're down on your knees." The result is that he hates her, while simultaneously loving her.

For most men, she is just the dearest Being, who gives good reason for being involved in the everyday struggle with outside obstacles. For some, who are artists, a woman is an inspiration, a topic of their creations, and the subject of admiration. For yet still another group of men, the object of their love is also perceived as a guide into worlds unattainable by any other means.

Horacio, the hero of Cortazar's *Hopscotch* says (p. 99): *The true otherness made up of delicate contacts, marvelous adjustment with the world, could not be attained from just one point, the outstretched hand had to find response in another hand stretched out from the beyond, from the other part.*

Freedom and Roles to Be Played

One of the possible definitions of freedom could be based on its connection with time. From such a perspective, freedom would be the time given to us to manage in an environment that does not impose on us its dimension of time. We have as much freedom as we can exercise, independent from the protocol of the environment in which we exist. In a more general version of this definition, we could say that freedom is the interval between a flash of duration and the sound of silence, given to us to manage in an environment that does not impose on us its dimension of tenure on earth.

As we have already mentioned, time is closely connected with the intimacy of experiencing. Love is an unusual (because desirable) interference into the most personal (because the least controlled by others) time and space of another person. For such interference one pays the highest price: the price of losing personal freedom. In love, a desire for sharing exceeds the desire for being, understood as a possibility of using one's own freedom. We surrender to a savory slavery.

Gottfried Wilhelm von Leibnitz believed that *to love is to place our happiness in the happiness of another.* Should we, however, be surprised with human longing for intensification—in its essence a doubling, completing, fulfilling our highest, most private freedom through the highest, most personal freedom of our loved one?

Marriage creates possibilities for the full realization of the concept of the ideal contact through sharing, and in fact, in many cases it fulfills this ideal. Nevertheless, the number of divorces indicates that implementation of this idea may be quite difficult. The main factors that make it uneasy are the strictness and canons (rules, models, or concepts) that come to life at the moment the contact between the lovers is institutionalized. The environment called *family* is a creation of spouses, both for, and against them. Once established, it imposes roles on their creators and obligates them to fulfill these roles.

For most couples, marriage constitutes what for lovers was an eternal uncertainty and waiting. But is certainty better than uncertainty? Of course, most people want assurance, to fulfill their ambitions and their views of the world. Yes, uncertainty is painful. But in certain ways, uncertainty is also more delectable than certainty. Some spouses, when they are sure (thinking that they know), think they know the future and that it is guaranteed. So, they may relax in that believed certainty, relieved to think there is no need for them make the effort to care any longer. This means that they may lose their sensitivity, their readiness, their *state of alertness* to the relationship.

For some unfortunate couples, marriage is understood as a guarantee of something that should in fact be the object of constant care. In such cases, an awareness of being married may compromise the instinct of sensitivity, sometimes it may terminate desire for experiencing the most intimate freedom: managing together the territory of time in a way that is controlled neither by environment, by strictness, by protocol to be followed—nor by the roles that are to be played.

Once some people have experienced the triumphal sensation that their partners "belong" to them, they are inclined to exercise, at least occasionally, the self-granted rights of the possessors.

D. H. Lawrence in his *The Escaped Cock* went as far as stating that *there was no contact without a subtle attempt to inflict a compulsion* (page 34).

It seems that in addition to longing for contact, or because, as a popular song states, *everybody needs somebody to lean on,* many people are looking for ways of inflicting compulsion. Or, paraphrasing the above quotation almost everybody needs somebody to compel.

Loneliness of the Two

Deep in human nature, the desire for contact comes from unhappy solitude. Contact is a break in loneliness and upholds the never-ending hope for an experience of true understanding.

Language carefully indicates delicate but decisive contrast, distinguishing *aloneness* from *loneliness*. A person who is alone does not have to be lonesome. Sometimes we need to be alone, and we choose solitude. We can be cloistered in complete silence and still not feel grief.

To feel lonely, we do not have to be left alone. Loneliness can be fully experienced among others and the number of people who surround us is of no importance. We can suffer significantly from friendly, superficial chats when that is all there are; when nothing is said that really means something to us. The parade of mouths moving with unrelenting empty meanings only deepens our sense of detachment. So, why don't we withdraw from this? Because most of us prefer a loneliness in which one is not alone.

Of course, we do not want to feel lonely and we look, sometimes desperately, for somebody to ease our suffering. But loneliness is something more than the lack of another person. Unhappy solitude means that we lack another person who understands us and whom we understand, and this is a precondition of not suffering from loneliness. Thus, to be together with somebody, does not necessarily mean we avoid loneliness. Two who are each lonely, simply juxtaposed one to the other, do not especially become two happy people. On the contrary, the presence of somebody who does not appeal to our intimate sense of contact can only deepen our stress. Recovery from the sadness caused by spiritual solitude is not possible without reciprocal understanding from a partner.

Communication Without Contact

When true contact between her and him ceases to exist, communication becomes a game in which both sides try to obtain their goals or at least to communicate them. They have to communicate, even when it is painful. *One cannot **not** communicate*, wrote Paul Watzlawick in his *An Anthology of Human Communication*. Of course, one could argue that sometimes, when we do not want to, we do not talk. It is true, but by *not* talking we communicate that we are withdrawing from communication, because we do not like the particular communicative situation and we refuse to participate, or for instance, we just do not know what to say, because we are ashamed, or too ignorant, or perhaps because we are too proud.

Skillful communicators believe that by saying something in a certain way they cause a certain reaction in the people with whom they converse. As the title of the J. L. Austin book says, they try to *do things with words*. In fact, there are several ways in which one can communicate a message: (1) *referential, direct:* asking somebody to do something formulating it in a direct way, e.g., "keep away from boys if you want to finish your freshman year," "take an umbrella," (2) *referential, indirect:* an attempt not to hurt the pride of those being advised, by use of camouflaged form: "you should now concentrate only on your studies," "it is going to rain," and (3) *non-referential, veiled:* neither direct nor indirect reference to the genuine intention of the sender; usually it appeals to a more general area in which the real intention is included: "Your father's greatest dream is that you graduate one day from college," "you should take good care of yourself."

Let us take a look at the invented situation in which one partner of communication uses linguistic manipulation to obtain his communicative aim:

CIRCUMSTANCES: there are two persons involved, a husband and a wife. She is going out. He has just returned home, so he knows that there is an unbearably cold breeze outside. He notices that his wife is wearing a T-shirt. He would like her to dress in a heavier outfit, but he knows that he cannot transmit his wish to her directly. They experience some communicative difficulties: e.g., she has a serious problem with him telling her what to do. Even when it does refer to a minor, insignificant matter, as a rule, she will not follow his advice. It could have something to do with his dominating personality, maybe with his autocratic tendencies; the fact is that they have reached the point in which his advice to her is almost always ignored.

HIS STRATEGY: knowing the domestic communicative pattern, he will not try to act directly. Instead, he will attempt to send his message in as neutral way as possible. An order, a request, a suggestion, these would not work. By saying "take your sweatshirt" he would ensure that she would catch a cold that night. That is why he decides to say only "it's going to be very cold tonight."

DESIRABLE RESULT: When he gets as a response "Oh, really? Maybe I should take my sweatshirt?" he has almost reached his goal, unless he says: "yes, this is what you should have done from the very beginning" or "at last you appreciate advice from someone more responsible than yourself!" then... a failure. But suppose everything went well, according to his expectations, and he had already heard "maybe I should take a sweatshirt?" What should he do? The best advice is *silence:* yes, the best way is to say nothing, leaving the impression that it was her own idea, and that he did not interfere with what she should wear that evening.

ACTUAL RESULT: The couple under discussion has a serious communication difficulty. If they were able to communicate successfully, they would not have to use linguistic manipulation. To be a skillful manipulator one has to be a sober, cool player. In such a game, emotion is the worst enemy. What can happen next, after her declaration of what we understand is his victory for the sake of protecting her from catching cold? Emotions are entering the scene. He, being happy with his victory and being seduced by the temptation of celebrating his success, decides to say something else. For example, for the sake of stressing his smartness he says "come on, don't exaggerate, it is not as cold as you imagine" (and in his heart he believes that he strengthened his victorious proposal). As usual, in such cases he believes that the only creature on this earth that thinks is he himself, and this is why he can so easily trick others. But his wife, annoyed and maybe even harmed by his "lesson," either because she realized that he manipulated her or because she was capricious that day, says: "forget it, it is hot enough to go *only* in a T-shirt."

WHO IS THE LOSER? AND A WORD ON HIM AND HER: From the moment she adds this, the fact that he is in fact the loser in this situation becomes obvious. Whatever else is true here, the pain caused by her independence is something that he experiences, perhaps in addition to an overwhelming feeling of jealousy: how many times did he mention to her that in a T-shirt, in his judgment, she had a provocative appearance and could have been exposed to unpleasant sexual comments or advances from male strangers...?

But is he the only loser in this communication?

In general, all people use various communicative strategies in interaction with their loved ones. The problem of the couple just described lies beyond the addiction to linguistic manipulation.

She and he were unable to use direct communication because they were no longer partners in contact. She hated him telling her what to do; he could not tell her that he was jealous. Nonetheless, together, both of them were living out communicative loneliness.

The Undisclosed and the Irretrievable Contacts

First a person loses his heart. Nothing may next happen if we do not let the person we fell head over heels in love with know about it. And, after all, there are many reasons for not communicating affection; so what are some possible causes preventing an effective attempt to establish contact despite longing for it?

There is the type of communicators who regularly present themselves to the world as the tough individuals. They build a solid self-image of the independent, self-reliant, and emotionally self-supporting persons. They sacrifice a lot to construct a monument of self and they are not ready to expose it to external unpredictable stimuli. The owner of the carefully nurtured self-phantom cannot afford its exposure to the test that may result in rejection from the approached person. Denial would mean deep scratches on the polished but insecure sense of well-being and adequacy, a form of vanity.

There are people confused by endless doubts. The uncertain sand-like castle-builders suffer from the paralysis of indecision. Never sure, undiscovered but definite jewels, always expecting the arrival of a prince, they believe that those who have declared their fondness to them so far are not worthy to be initiated into the idealized lands somewhere in the clouds.

And there are legions of silent visitors to the valley of tears, harmed in unfortunate affairs, too vulnerable to risk another cataclysm. Some of those among the wounded wear the masks of cynics, being ashamed of their defenselessness. Cynical opinions expressed by them, which scorn or even vulgarize relationships between her and him, hide the fear of being rejected again, or even more troublesome—of being ridiculed. Even the strongest individuals are unprotected from being mocked—the most devastating harm done to an ego.

First we lose our hearts. Sometimes we are swept off our feet immediately—hence, magic or strong chemistry is involved. Then, usually, we love even more. If we let the objects of our affections know our feelings and uncover that we are loved too, we may find a common world, build an intimacy of contact, and adore our partner more deeply in return for simply being our companion.

Later, one day, we may find that we are indifferent, apathetic—suddenly—as quickly and suddenly as when we had earlier fallen in love.

Surprisingly, however, it does not have to mean that the former beloved is abandoned. We may stay with our partners due to the habituation, loyalty, devotion, pity, fear of being lonely, or because of the need for preservation of a contact, even if it is an imperfect one. It may also happen that a relationship is broken off for good as a result of disillusionment with a partner or with self; the relationship, i.e., allowed us to discover nuances of which we were previously unaware. Because of overestimation, or the burden of responsibility for the other person that we are not able, or do not want to bear, we withdraw from an earlier-established contact.

Sometimes we love desperately, regardless of what we have discovered about our partner, against common sense, and we love even after losing respect for the person. It looks as if we were doomed from the start to become a slave to love, incomprehensible to the surrounding world, betrayed, humiliated, beaten, and even when finally separated from him or her, deep in our heart we are still in love with this important person.

For many, when they face a loss of a partner, the reaction is a dramatic attempt to rescue the relationship. Again, as irrationally and obsessively, determinedly and passionately, as when it possessed us for the first time, we behave when love tries, against our will, to escape from us.

The hero of a film *Without Anesthesia*, by Andrzej Wajda, the famous Polish film director, after returning home from abroad, finds that his wife has left him and is living with somebody else. He begs her to return but she refuses. He then asks their common friend to mediate and to deliver to his wife a letter requesting her homecoming. His friend is upset with the self-humiliating way the man is handling the crisis, and tries to appeal to his self-respect and pride. "Damn the pride"—the man answers—"this is my life!"

Of course, it is possible to convince, or even to force a partner to stay, but no one can be forced to love, and this man knows it well.

When in the last scene of the film an explosion consumes his home and him as well, it is clear that this man's hope was built on his faith in his ability to build a meaningful contact with at least one other person—a hope that had actually been completely burned and ended emotional eons before his body perished in the flames.

FOURTH LONGING: CONTACT WITH STRANGERS

Total Inadequacy

Imagine: one day you find yourself working for the U.S. Army as a military officer. You have a general knowledge about the army, but you have never gone through military training. You understand a little from the military language that is used by your fellow officers. They know that you are new and they are ready to give you a hand but they have no idea about the extent of your ignorance.

Or imagine that your been chosen to be a part of a free-style relay in a high school meet and you can barely swim.

Or that your advanced professional license has been revoked, your degree ignored, and you were told to start college on a freshman level.

Or that you are an immigrant who has recently arrived to the U.S.A.

So what happens to you at the beginning of any of these new journeys?

At the first stage, *confusion* dominates over all other feelings. Suddenly, after years of existential silence, you are facing the very basic ontological questions:

Where am I?
What am I doing here?
Is this a place for me?

You are surrounded by a strange environment in which people do not share your values and beliefs, and use a language that you may know but you are not comfortable with it. You feel that you are living inside a movie, like an actor who has to follow the orders of an eccentric film-director.

Despite of strange things that are happening to you, you are struggling to survive. Imagine now your reaction to the stress that you are constantly experiencing.

After a busy and stressing day, finally at home, which is a shelter from the alien world outside, after a drink or two, you fall asleep and you're back—to the city in your homeland where you used to live, and to the language that you are longing for. In this way, you return to your inborn normality. Even if it was a quite abnormal normality as in the case of living under communism.

And then you wake up and you are facing the same strange reality you left behind you the day before. No doubt, you are caught in what we know as an identity crisis.

Identity Crisis, or, Not HERE, Not NOW; Who Am I?

Let us consider for a moment this confused state of mental affairs. I believe that the following triad of words:
$$I - HERE - NOW$$
in a simple way describe our points of reference in the Universe:

The element "I" distinguishes between the person speaking (or thinking in language) and the others, who might be marked by pronouns "you," "she," and "he."

The element "here" allows differentiating from another location marked by the element "there."

Finally, the element "now" separates the present moment from the past and the future ("before" and "later").

Aberrations from the presented order usually indicate certain unusual phenomena in interpretation of self and reality. For example when "I" means also "you" or "she," we could be dealing with multiple personality disorder, borderline personality structure, or with schizophrenia.

When the spatial element "here" becomes exchangeable with "there," or when the temporal factor "now" becomes "before," this can indicate hallucinations, delusions, or a schizophrenic process.

My general assumption is that in a case of the immigrant experience, the elements of the triad
$$I - HERE - NOW$$
undergo dramatic change, taking a form of the new triad
$$I - Not\ HERE - Not\ NOW$$
or, simply:
$$I - THERE - BEFORE.$$

In other words, the immigrant's identity is based on earlier spatial and temporal experience. What happens then to a person who experiences such a state of mind?

Contact

Despite of the existential confusion, the immigrant has to live with it and to act according to the demands of the surrounding environment. The external world is not aware of the true points of reference of immigrants. What they are forced to do, is, in fact, to lead a *double life:* OVER HERE *and* OVER THERE; NOW *and* BEFORE—all simultaneously!

Eva Hoffman illustrated this phenomenon aptly in her book *Lost in Translation: A life in a New Language* (pp. 199-200):

> *Should you become a pianist? the question comes in English.*
>
> *No, you mustn't. You can't.*
>
> *Should you become a pianist? the question echoes in Polish.*
>
> *Yes, you must. At all costs.*
>
> *The costs will be too high.*
>
> *The costs don't matter. Music is what you're meant to do.*
>
> *Don't be so dramatic. I can play for myself. For pleasure.*
>
> *Don't kid yourself. You want to play for others. You want to hear the applause.*
>
> *That's a shallow ideal.*
>
> *It's those eyes when people have heard you play...*
>
> *I'm going to end up giving concerts in small towns and colleges. There are too many pianists in the world going over the same tired repertory. What can I add to all those recordings of the Chopin études?*
>
> *Reasons, reasons... You're passionate about it....You have a duty to yourself.*
>
> *I live here now. I can't just close my eyes and follow my passions; I have to figure out how to live my life.*
>
> *Oh God, I don't know. I don't know what you should do anymore.*
>
> *I like literature a lot. I'm good at it. Perhaps someday I can write. Sometimes, I almost get the same high...*
>
> *Not the same. Nothing expresses as much. What else will you love like that?*
>
> *I'll love other things. I'll love people. I promise.*

> *Remember how you felt...*
> *No. I don't want to remember.*
> *What do you want? What do you want?*
> *I want ... I want not to have to change so much. But I have to. I have to catch up to myself. It's not just a question of music, you know.*
> > *Yes, I know. But it's going to hurt, giving it up.*
> > *Yes, it's going to hurt.*
> > *But we'll get along somehow.*
> > *Yes, we'll get along.*

What are the prospects for Eva's adaptation process? I would say: good.

And the reason for this guess is her highly self-psychotherapeutic intuition. Eva has obtained two important goals when it comes to overcoming her crisis: she identified the source of the inner conflict and prescribed a therapy for herself based on existential considerations: life may be painful, it leaves scars on us, and it creates no opportunity for escaping from taking responsibility for it: *Yes, it's going to hurt. But we'll get along somehow.*

The example quoted refers to experiences of a Polish-American immigrant, but has a universal value. Eva's internal struggles are typical of numbers of immigrants from various cultural environments, as the following example of Rose, the Chinese client in therapy described by Stanley Messer, shows:

> She talks about how she can only curse in English, not Chinese, and that she never confronted her parents or disobeyed them because of her conception of what it was to be a daughter in a Chinese family. She feels there are two sides of her: the Chinese side, which is passive, obedient, holds back feeling, and the like, and the "social" side, which can get angry at men because she trusts them more than women.
>
> Stanley B. Messer and C. Seth Warren,
> *Models of Brief Psychodynamic Therapy*, p. 190.

The fragment just quoted clearly shows that in addition to an identity crisis, the immigrant has to face at least two more crises: the value crisis and the communication crisis.

Value Crisis and Communication Crisis:
The East/Central European Case Study

In the widest sense, we are considering here a conflict between the European and the American values. In the more narrow sense, it would be the conflict between Central European and American values. In the most narrow sense, it might be a conflict between Polish and American values. The typical Polish national slogan "God - Honor - Homeland" illustrates it in an apt way. The saying translates into the demand that one should protect his or her homeland; if necessary to fight for her; and if needed, to sacrifice life for her. As Maria Janion formulated it in *Wampir*, from this perspective the homeland appears as a vampire sucking the blood of her citizenry. Another assumption is that those Poles who emigrated are traitors because they "left" their homeland. The citizens of Switzerland or France can *choose* to live in Canada or the USA; a Pole, according to this system of thinking *cannot*. Let me add one more, stress-causing feature, typical of Polish-American immigrants, namely the question that has to be often confronted by them: "what did you do for Poland?" and the presumption is that the emigrant has stopped "doing things for Poland" on the day Poland was left behind.

A more trivial example can be taken from the field of holiday celebrations, especially Christmas. The difference between Polish and American ways is that the Americans anticipate this holiday, and the Poles commemorate it. In other words, in the USA, the Christmas tree is decorated in early December and thrown out just after December 25; the Polish tradition was (because it's changing now, with progressing process of "MacDonaldization" of Poland) to decorate the tree on Christmas Day and to keep it almost to the end of the January. Typical immigrants would have a tendency to follow traditions, which were brought from the homeland, unless their children start to demand an adjustment. The pressure from them is to adjust the time of decoration of the tree to the practices of the American, neighboring houses. I would say that the Polish adaptation to the U.S. could be measured by the progress in the number of days before Christmas that the Polish immigrant agrees to decorate the tree.

The examples quoted here, despite their specific ethnic source, have more universal value, typical of the smaller, European nations (especially in post-communist times), which show similar tendencies when it comes to dealing with immigration. Milan Kundera, himself an émigré from Czechoslovakia, in his book *Testaments Betrayed*, indicates that in the language of the smallest European nation, the Icelanders, the term *family* means 'a multiple obligation,' and another term, *family ties* translates into no more and no less than 'the cords of multiple obligation.' Following the small nation's semantic and emotional sensitivity towards the concept of homeland as a family, the author of *The Unbearable Lightness of Being* mentions the endless embroilment in obligations towards the homeland typical of a writer who originates from a small country. This kind of emotional involvement is so strong that practically it excludes a possibility of the "sinless" departure from the old country.

When Nietzsche mercilessly criticized the German national character or Stendhal announced that he had preferred Italy over his own homeland, no German or Frenchman took offense. But, as Kundera indicates, if something like this should have happened to a Greek or Czech, then such a writer would be denounced by his national "family" as a dreadful traitor. What is typical for small nations is their cultivation of a warm intimacy within which everybody watches everybody and jealousy is omnipotent. Kundera quotes Gide's words:

> Families, I hate you! ... There is nothing more dangerous for you than *your own* family, *your own* room, *your own* past... You must leave them ... *Ibsen, Strindberg, Joyce, Seferis knew this. They spent a larger part of their lives abroad, away from the family's power.*
>
> Milan Kundera, *Testaments*, p.194.

All of the above-presented characteristics may lead to guilty feelings which when added to an identity confusion, does not help the immigrant in process of assimilation to the new environment.

The third crisis is a communication crisis. I once participated in a conference on European affairs. The conference was conducted in English. When the floor was open for comments from the audience, a man stood up and said in English that according to his wife, when he speaks Polish, he sounds like a bright, eloquent, highly educated gentleman, while when he speaks English, he creates an impression of rather primitive and ignorant person. The rest of the comments by this Polish-American businessman were delivered in Polish.

One of my Jewish American friends told me a story about her and her sister who emigrated from Poland in the '60s to the US and to Israel. One of the sisters learned English but did not know Hebrew; another one learned Hebrew but had no chance to study English. Forty years have passed and the sisters were still using Polish in their correspondence.

A Croatian-born American psychotherapist reported to me that she had a significant number of Polish-American clients. "Do you speak Polish?" I asked her. "No," she answered, "My clients talk to me in English. But they feel that I understand what they are talking about, because I am from Europe."

To understand and to be understood are two prerequisites of communication. Without knowledge of language the immigrants are sentenced to isolation in their ethnic ghetto. Language, when it is not understood, may become a significant source of frustration or even may lead to mental dysfunction. No wonder that the immigrants are among the two population groups that have the highest risk of developing paranoia; the second group is that of hearing-impaired people.

Of course successful communication requires much more than the knowledge of the language. The immigrant who is willing to assimilate must not only learn the language but adjust his perception of reality according to the new language. To do this, he has to change the habits of his heart.

The process of assimilation in the new environment is of complex character and is a reflection of the relation between the new HERE and NOW and the old one. Or the relation between the two factors: Assimilation and Ethnic Identity.

The Four Ways of Dealing with the Immigrant Experience

I would like to focus now on relation between Assimilation and Ethnic Identity. Let us consider the model that was inspired by John Berry's "Acculturation as varieties of adaption":

ASSIMILATION HIGH

ETHNIC IDENTITY LOW	*ETHNIC IDENTITY HIGH*
Assimilationists Negative view of own culture, attempt to assimilate at any price, use of English (even broken) at home with elimination of native language, attempt to minimize the influence of the ethnic culture and customs. Live according to the pattern: **I-HERE-NOW**	**Integrationists** Positive view of majority culture and respect for won culture. Live according to the pattern: **I-HERE enriched by THERE-NOW enriched by BEFORE**
ETHNIC IDENTITY LOW	*ETHNIC IDENTITY HIGH*
ETHNIC IDENTITY LOW	*ETHNIC IDENTITY HIGH*
Marginal people Hold negative view of both majority culture and own culture: the old was lost, the new was not found. Live according to the pattern: **(Not) I - Not HERE/THERE - Not NOW/BEFORE**	**Separatists (Traditionalists)** Are obedient to own customs and traditions and have a negative view of new, majority culture. Live according to the pattern: **I - THERE – BEFORE**
ETHNIC IDENTITY LOW	*ETHNIC IDENTITY HIGH*

ASSIMILATION LOW

Assimilationists

Immigrants from this category wish they were born in the U.S. Their real life started the moment they had first touched the American soil. They are ashamed of their roots and want to forget about it completely. When possible, they change their first and last names, cut off contacts with family members in the old country and when being (unfortunately) asked, "where are you from?" (one cannot get rid of his accent)—they try not to answer. A lot of effort is put on the careful imitation of American traditions, which they adopt with great devotion to the point of being holier than the Pope. They are quick in harsh criticism of their former country and fellow compatriots and uncritical in praising the United States according to the slogan "everything is the best in America." Their unshakable positive thinking about the new country reminds one of Pollyanna, the heroine of a book with that name by Eleanor H. Porter.

The model the Assimilationists represent is not the most grounded and effective one, because a creative and productive life requires not only wings but roots as well. In addition, disowning one's origin often leads to unconscious guilty feelings.

Separatists

We meet them on the other end of the spectrum. As everything American is perfect for Assimilationists, for Separatists it is the worst. They suffer from a superiority complex, believing that American values, education, culture, etc., are not in a position to compete with those of the immigrants' country of origin. But, as it is the case with complexes, the feeling of inferiority feeds on a lack of security, on an unconscious or hidden inferiority complex. There is an immigrant from East/Central Europe—like a hick from the provinces from the perspective and context of his life in America—who, a little scared and a bit embarrassed with the shameless luxury of American wealth, tries to compensate his embarrassment by depreciation of American values. Here the old country compared to America is seen as economically poorer but spiritually richer, technologically backward but smarter, not so monumental and imperial, but having a deep Slavic soul—this immigrant uses a counterpoint comparative vision as a defense mechanism.

Many immigrants, but especially the Traditionalists, have a tendency to repeat the behaviors typical of the old country in a new environment. Unfortunately, what was working OVER THERE will not be effective HERE. Hopeless attempts of repeating the learned behaviors in the new context are ineffective and stress-building. The injured I suffers from low self-esteem. Such a feeling is a reflection of the real or assumed lack of respect coming from the outside world. Deprivation of positive, external stimuli intensifies the attempts to transmit THERE to the U.S., already doomed to failure, and the mechanism of a vicious circle starts to operate.

Emotional difficulties may undergo somatization after a while. There was a case of an immigrant from Bosnia-Herzegovina, living in metropolitan Detroit who would regularly call emergency almost weekly during a full one year because of acute pain in his chest. The results of medical examinations were always the same — there were no signs of cardiovascular disease. There was no trace of past heart problems in the medical history of this elder gentleman, either. Pain regularly experienced by him had an exclusively existential background. (Based on a recounting by therapist Maria Dixon, personal communication, 1999.)

Marginal People

There are people who would never find themselves in a new reality. However what is special about them is that they did not belong to the previous one either. They were outsiders in their homeland and it was their choice. The former culture, traditions, and sense of belonging or unity were not appealing to them. In the new environment they remain similarly silent and detached. Małgorzata Warchoł-Schlottmann aptly describes such a person: *The marginal man stands on the edge of two worlds: a part of both, but a partner in neither, a man caught between two cultures, two languages and feeling at home in neither.* ("The disintegrative personality of a Pole in Germany," p. 33)

If in the case of previous two formations there was an opportunity for fulfillment (regardless its partial or even illusive nature), the representatives of this category will not find satisfaction or consolation. Why is that so? The answer is simple – the source of their misery lies not outside but inside them and no external condition can change it.

Integrationists

Among the four presented models, only this one is optimal. In this type of immigrant attitude, one connects a positive perception of a new culture with a respect towards that of a country of origin. They present the most stimulating approach that Danuta Mostwin called the Third Value. The Third Value is a combination of the two sources of culture, and in this way equips an immigrant in both: roots and wings. Given that an average immigrant comes from a country with a much more challenging environment that the U.S., in a natural way he or she is predestined to succeed in a new country. The Integrationists have the best chance to utilize talents they brought with them by using the opportunities to be found in America.

Adjusting to the New Country

Emotional confusion, even chaos, is a natural reaction to a person that has to adjust two crucial points of reference—HERE and NOW—simultaneously. Before the new is built, there is a time of a vacuum that might be filled with feelings of self-doubting and low self-esteem, to the point of despairing. That is why immigrants would benefit from the knowledge about the complex and painful process of fine-tuning to the new HERE and NOW. Understanding of a problem is a precondition to dealing with it. It seems that the immigrant's path towards a productive assimilation would be less bumpy if a newcomer to the U.S. was aware that the disintegrative process in which the immigrant experiences crises in self-perception, communication and systems of value is inevitable and normal, expected, and perfectly OK.

Once the understanding is accomplished, an attempt should be made to turn the disintegration into a positive track. Polish psychologist, Kazimierz Dąbrowski formulated the theory of positive disintegration, in which he stated that disintegrative processes are painful but necessary steps in achieving higher level of self-realization.

Using plain language and trivial examples, we can describe an early immigrant experience as "being under construction." To make it more comprehensible, imagine that you commute everyday on a very congested two-lane road. Finally, the city decides to build a third lane. You are delighted about the prospects of having no traffic. But wait a minute — before it happens, it will be even worse for long months: one of the two lanes will be blocked... Or, think about remodeling your bathroom and installing a Jacuzzi hot-tub there. There will a price to pay, and a part of it will be your inconvenience of not being able to use the bathroom for the time being... Or think about jumping up. The lower you bend before doing it, the higher you get....

For immigrants it should mean that in their *second life* (this is what the experiences of emigration involve) the immigrants, instead of dropping their unique ways of acting, feeling and understanding, should just modify them, keeping them alive but within the new framework. In this way, certain specific psychological features of most immigrants, like tendency to revolt against the situation in which fate has put them, the use of extra-systemic ways of thinking, or abilities to survive in difficult and hostile environment, could all be turned to the advantage of these people. Of course, there is no way to avoid certain negative aspects of going through the process of immigration. As I have mentioned, to be an immigrant means to have a "second life" but it also means to teethe, to learn how to walk and how to speak one more time.

I am convinced that there is as urgent need for counseling services for immigrants. It is a vital American interest to address this need and to help immigrants to become satisfied, successful, and productive American citizens.

Which schools of psychotherapy seem to be the most useful here? I believe that the Adlerian school of individual psychology (Alfred Adler, *The Practice and Theory of Individual Psychology*) in which he stresses the need of becoming all what we can become, and striving for the most we can be—rather that striving for to being "normal"—would be a useful inspiration for the counselors dealing with the immigrants population. According to Adler, every person wants to grow, expand, reach beyond the horizon, become above average, strive for achieving the upper ranges, and this is perfectly attainable for immigrants. What is more, immigrants seem to be especially predestined to such an experience. Why is this so? Because the immigrant who wants to survive in the new environment is simply forced to do so.

Another source of inspiration that could be used in counseling services for immigrants could be the existential school, which makes use of the following principles:

1. Recognizing that life is at times unfair and unjust
2. Recognizing that ultimately there is no escape from some of life's life's pain (...)
3. Learning that I must take ultimate responsibility for the way I live my life no matter how much guidance and support I get from others.

Irvin Yalom, *The Theory and Practice of Group Psychotherapy*, p. 88.

The immigrant is in position to fully experience fully the existential challenges presented by life. A counselor canshould make their clients aware that those challenges are not disadvantages, but their chances.

Peripheries of Contact: War and Occupation

The opposite of immigration, in which a newcomer is welcomed by a chosen country, is an invasion, when an arrival is not welcomed, and the one who is coming uninvited becomes an intruder. Instead of *hosting* a *guest*, *hostility* towards the *host* by the invaderof the enemies takes place. It is interesting to notice that the Latin root word for all these italicized terms is the same: *hostis*, meaning in Latin *stranger* or *foe*.

There is a historical background of this semantic paradox. Those, who were invited one time, refused to leave and turned to be parasites or simply occupying enemies. That is why the noun *guest* and the verb *hostile* have the same etymological origin. Twentieth-century history provides many examples of this semantic twist. For instance, the Soviet Red Army that in 1945 entered several countries in Europe in order to liberate them from the occupation by Nazi Germany occupation, forgot to leave them for the next forty-five years.

Invaders intend to extend their world beyond theirs border. The goal of expansion is to impose a new order based on the values of the aggressors. From the perspective of *contact*, we are dealing here with its deepest pathology, with its perversion.

We may compare this with the case of an immigrant, whose aim is to assimilate to the new environment. With an invader, we are dealing with the contradictory attempt: the goal of the conqueror is to subjugate the invaded strangers completely and to turn them into slaves.

Normal, two-channel communication, becomes a one-way pathway whose purpose is the transmission of the will of those who are in charge. The rulers are not interested in an exchange of information; they are looking for ways of imposing their plans. They represent a dictatorial authority based on fear that is inflicted by the use of coercive measures.

When it comes to governing based on despotic authority, called "irrational authority" by Erich Fromm, the 20th century delivers a rich variety of clinical examples for the students of the history of non-democratic, totalitarian governments; the century that started with communism was soon facing fascism; the tired century ended with the deadly, tribal nationalism of the Balkan Peninsula. With the birth of this new millennium, despite having witnessed earlier horrifying experiences, humanity hoped for the better future. But already at its dawn, we were numbed with the tragedy of September 11, 2001 (now known as 9/11). Another war is going on now: a war with terrorism.

And East/Central Europe after communism? The people were not dancing on the streets; they were confused, lost, and outraged by the merciless, cruel, undeveloped capitalism that replaced the welfare state. Instead of prosperity, for many it brought unemployment, new, non-state exploitation, or even homelessness. Pains outnumbered gains; the vacuum left by unfulfilled expectations was being filled by demagogy, populism, and scapegoating. The birth of democracy was not smooth at all, and did not occur without serious complications.

New Walls in People's Hearts or
Hope Isn't That Young Girl Anymore...

Almost a quarter century ago, in 1989, the fall of the Berlin wall seemed to mark not only the beginning of the end of Russian control over East-Central Europe, but perhaps for the first time in the 20th century, the start of a new epoch filled with hopes and expectations toward a better, safer, more just, and equal world. This great hope, filled with optimism, and marked by the unprecedented switch from a one-party to a multi-party system, awoke the world's imagination, giving birth to the anticipation of common freedom. The future seemed to be bright. Unfortunately, these quickly-aroused expectations died almost as fast as they were born. Because of Russia's fall, its role as Euro-Asian policeman became inoperative. And without policemen, chaos rises.

The war in former Yugoslavia that took place in the '90s of the last century showed that new freedom was to be experienced in separate, distinct ways by different nations. Newfound liberty was understood by some of them as a license to act irrespective of the rights of others to exercise their freedom. The separatism they experienced, which occurred with the absence of foreign dominance, turned into deadly nationalism; the agony of Bosnia and Herzegovina became the most tragic manifestation of tribal tendencies.

The pendulum of the mood of the masses swung quickly from one end of the spectrum, where the reign of a pan-national idea of imperial unity was effectively smashing any sign of nationalism, to the opposite end, where tribalism replaced reason. The former Yugoslavia is not an exception. In today's party-free Euro-Asia, there are a number of spots that have already become or can become a blood bath for tens of thousands of people.

Many tribesmen of the former republics of the Soviet Union were in a state of war or its civil equivalent; ethnic conflicts were rising among the nations of the Balkan Peninsula, which might be transformed into a full-scale Balkan war. Formally reunited Germany is experiencing serious social and ideological divisions. Confusion and an uncertain future cause the savagery that appeals to many young Germans.

In Western Europe, anti-immigrant sentiments are becoming stronger, nationalistic, and in many cases racist; parties are planning international coalitions within the European Union. The sad irony is that they are going to use the EU foundations to propagate their dangerous ideas, and any attempt to prevent this from happening is interpreted by them as an attack against democracy.

Should we be surprised? Hasn't the history of the past century taught us enough lessons?

Yes, it has, but we are still astonished. Human nature makes us optimistic, and our optimism is based on a heavy load of good will that outshines malevolence. But to be hopeful should not mean to be blind and to pretend that one does not see the seriousness of the recent ethnic cleansing tragedies occurring around the world. We know that these tribal demons were always present—and not only in Europe. In the U.S., racial tensions are still strong. In East-Central Europe since World War II, those demons were suppressed by Russia's imperial discipline, but now that the empire is gone, they are back.

Regardless of the reasons, we cannot escape from the reality of the increasing vulgarity of political and social life in post-communist Europe. The downfall of physical walls was accompanied by the raising of invisible, and thus more impregnable, walls in people's minds. There are the walls of nationalism and hatred, xenophobia and populism, the walls of social differences, and the wealth of nations. José Ortega y Gasset, describing the connections between separatist tendencies and the brutalization of social life, warned:

> *Civilization is before all, the will to live in common. A man is uncivilized, barbarian in in the degree in which he does not take others into account. Barbarism is the tendency to disassociation. Accordingly, all barbarous epochs have been times of human scattering...*
> José Ortega y Gasset, *The Revolt of the Masses*, p. 76.

In 1848, Marx, spokesman for the modern masses, started his *Communist Manifesto* with the words "a specter is haunting Europe—the specter of communism."

One hundred sixty-five years have passed and the one-party reign has gone went into hibernation, but the spirit of the multi-party system cannot be felt. Another specter is haunting Europe instead: the specter of barbarism.

Wisława Szymborska, a Polish Nobel Laureate in literature, wrote a poem "The Century's Decline," in which she laments over the tragedies of the 20th century which at its beginning awoke great expectations of ending human suffering coming from emotional domains like unhappiness, fears, and lies, as well as physical realms of hunger or wars, turned out to be the monstrous one.

Those who were planning to experience joy ended up finding that it was "a hopeless task" and that, in her words:

Hope
isn't that young girl anymore,
et cetera, alas.

> Wisława Szymborska. *View with a Grain of Sand: Selected Poems*, p 148.

Shouldn't we be more optimistic against all the odds? Shouldn't we follow Karl Popper's inspirational thought that if only enough people decided to do the right things, then goodness would prevail, changing our world for the better?

We can certainly try our best to avoid a cynical interpretation of history, but we cannot escape from pictures of Bosnia in agony, rising hatred for immigrants among European societies, and a progressing vulgarization of political life in the post-communist states, "et cetera, alas" (as Wisława Szymborska has just put it). Hope is tired, she's getting old, and she has been shrinking lately. Unfortunately, according the Scottish poet, Thomas Campbell, "Coming events cast their shadows before."

So what to do? What prescription should be offered to those who suffer from the side effects of freedom? I like the one that was formulated by Lord Thomas Babington Macaulay: *There is only one cure for the evils, which newly required freedom produces, and that is freedom.*

History repeats itself. The year was 1848—often called the Spring of Nations, the Year of Revolution. Shortly thereafter, the Russian philosopher Alexander Herzen (1812-1870), reviewed those failed revolutions in his book *From the Other Shore* (1855)— earlier published as *Vom anderen Ufer* (German, 1850) and as *S togo berega* (*С того берега*; Russian, 1855)—commenting in Chapter VI (Omnia Mea Mecum Porto):

> The death of the contemporary forms of social order ought to gladden rather than trouble the soul. But what is frightening is that the departing world leaves behind it not an heir, but a pregnant widow. Between the death of one and the birth of the other much water will flow by, a long night of chaos and desolation will pass.
>
> A. Herzen, *From the Other Shore*, p. 124.

To paraphrase Gustaw Herling-Grudziński, we can say that we know that just as well in the current year as Herzen did back in 1849.

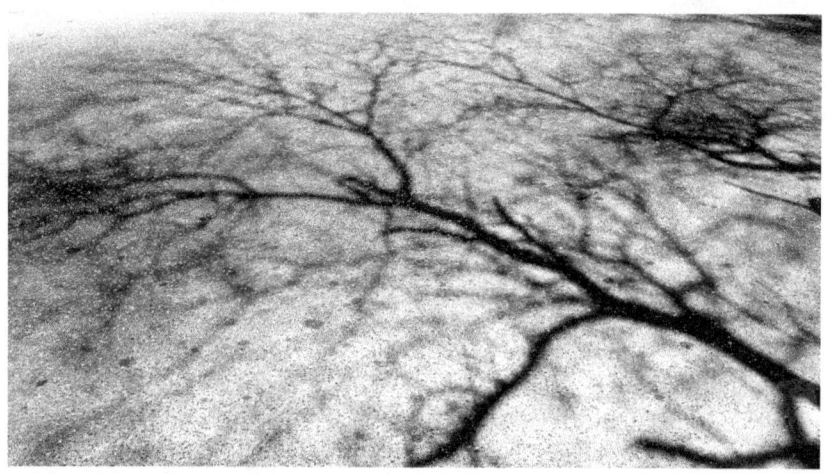

FIFTH LONGING:
CONTACT WITH YOURSELF
(FROM DICHOTOMY TO SYMBIOSIS)

The Curse of Egohood

This book tells a story of longing for contact. It describes how difficult it is to maintain an understanding, harmonious relationship and mutual tolerance among people, groups of them, and entire nations. When it comes to the conflict of opinions among people, it is more common that confrontation occurs rather than any party's giving up even the insignificant aspects of the beliefs, ideas, and ambitions that are involved in the specific disagreement. Lack of openness for others and for their points of views and needs is deeply rooted in the sense of individual identity so typical to a Western way of thinking and so rare in Eastern world.

While writing this book, I have noticed a symptomatic feature: it was much easier for me to come up with failures in communication rather than with successes. The reason is simple; the former, unfortunately, are more typical. The tragic paradox that is responsible for the miserable conditions of contact among people lies in contradiction between their longing for transcendence and the attachment to each's sense of self, the attachment to egohood. The more distinctive one wants to become, the less likely any achieving of unity with the universe and other people who are a part of it.

Before we continue our discussion, let us summarize the main concepts proposed so far in previous chapters:

1. Man is born without an awareness of his distinctiveness and is in an intuitive state of mind in which there is a natural connection between a newly-born person and the *essential source* (the Universe). Helen Palmer said this well:

> *as children we were connected to this essential source. However, with time, and because of the need to cope with the pressure of family life, children form a set of beliefs and habits that help them to survive.*
>
> Helen Palmer, "Introduction," in M. Stuart, *The Tarot*, p.VIII.

I believe that this set of beliefs is given to children through language. Language is also the best manifestation of these beliefs.

2. In addition, when a child is presented with language, he starts to realize that the mother is a different person, that his name is unique, and consequently, he distinguishes himself from other children and adults. The basic antinomy: *I ≠ world* is formed at this stage. The irony here is that the same language that is responsible for the conceptual isolation of its user (which may ultimately lead to complete loneliness), simultaneously delivers the most advanced tool for communication that can bring about overcoming man's loneliness.

3. When a child is older, he receives contradictory signals concerning his uniqueness: adults award him for distinguishing himself from other children by means of good grades and proper behavior (what allows the adults to differentiate themselves from others when they report that their child was admitted to a prestigious university and was granted with a full scholarship); his peers award him for uniformity in terms of average grades and not-so-good behavior.

4. In adulthood, the above-mentioned contradiction usually is overcome by the "superficial distinctiveness" that will be discussed later.

5. There are people, nevertheless, who do not accept such a state of experienced separateness from the universe, and attempt to achieve oneness with it.

In this chapter I will address certain aspects of contacts that most individuals make with themselves. If our longing for the restoration of the transcendent unity with the universe that was lost in our early childhood is to be fulfilled, several prerequisites must be met.

The following are some of these, which we will discuss in greater detail below: understanding our obsession with individuality, comprehending the dual nature of the Western conceptual world, establishing awareness of the paradoxical character of problems connected with certainty, recognizing the choices we make and the freedom we exercise, and finally, finding peace with ourselves.

Uniqueness and Unity: The Two Basic Longings

Western culture might be characterized as the culture of differences, not similarities. Much if not most of Western society puts significant effort into processes that ultimately are aimed at having people distinguish themselves from others. One's individuality is measured by one's level of distinctiveness from other human beings. Extreme chauvinism, deadly nationalism, or ethnic cleansing—all come from the same root of intolerance that is also called distinctiveness.

It seems that a lot of human activities are directed by two contradictory tendencies: the need to be distinct and the need to overcome loneliness that results from a successful quest for uniqueness. Other human beings are the ultimate criterion for the quality of these two longings. When one is satisfied with the distinctiveness being experienced, other people can confirm one's feeling of importance and pride. When one's uniqueness becomes a burden and a source of loneliness, another human being is the one who brings comfort through love, acceptance, and compassion. That is why most people make themselves available as subjects of constant emotional exchange with other human beings. Awards are sometimes enormous, but also the risk involved is high because an exchange may lead to use and abuse of the particular individuals interacting with one another. Nevertheless, a promise of a satisfying return is so seductive that the vast majority of people are addictive gamblers in this exchange.

Contacts with others describe our condition on the earth. We perceive the world through them. Power, money, and fame, and, on the other hand, misery and helplessness, are quite relative, because their quality is established by comparison with the life conditions of other people. These create a filter that structures most information that we absorb about our position in our world.

An average person emphasizes his individuality as often as possible. Being marked by the basic antinomy $I \neq World$, people use their intellect, talents, social power, authority, and sometimes also a physical force to show how significantly *different* they are from others.

Let us take a look for a moment at the particular features of our life that support our efforts to be different: consider the drive for a successful career and related ambitions for what we take to be significant material goods: where and what we live in, what we drive, what we wear, how good students our children are, and even where we spend our leisure time and at how much a cost—all those features can be used to distinguish one given person from others. But do these efforts really lead to expected goals?

Do these endeavors actually guide us to a desert island, of which we would be the only inhabitant? The answer is: no.

Hopes for fulfilling ambitions within the above-described categories are driven by one's desire to equal others in what they are "better" than one is. But instead of distinguishing oneself, one in fact tries to identify with a more, according to his categories, elitist group. Actually, one looks for the *uniform distinction* in which exclusiveness is the primary category of success. The unpleasant truth is that the striving for uniqueness by means of "having" will never fully satisfy one's appetite. Why? Because the compulsive accumulation of goods, money, honor, fame, or power will lead to an even-deeper division between the one who gained a lot and those who did not. The solitude of a millionaire who barricades himself behind thick protective walls may eliminate a chance for contact with others. Consequently, such a lack of contact will only empower this person's tendency to multiply power. At this stage, the unfulfilled goal of obtaining contact with the external world may switch to its opposite, to giving up on this very need that becomes a source of pain instead of satisfaction. The attempt to be distinct typically moves toward multiplication of material power. If one is born in a well-to-do family, he may look for uniqueness by the rejection of materialism and a critical attitude toward the way of life typical of the establishment. Escape to originality or eccentricity here would take a form of unification with those who own less rather than more. Sometimes, longing for true contact is suppressed, because one is afraid of its unpredictability, its depth, and its requirements of openness and intimacy. Another fear—as in the case of escaping from love—would be the fear of being ridiculed in case of betrayal, when contact has failed and left one wounded and vulnerable. Fear is stronger than longing. Coexistence seems to be more challenging than competition. In true contact, one faces possibility of discovering that his egohood or self-identity is actually neither as separated nor as unique as it had earlier seemed to be.

The feeling of unity with another person is the beginning of a journey in which one can be driven beyond his own boundaries to the territory where the world built on the system of opposites so eminent to us would be melted. Among those thawed oppositions there would be the basic one, which was responsible for the birth of all the others. In the moment of such unity, one would stop being in an antagonistic relation to everything around: on the contrary, the formula *I ≠ world*, would become the equation *I = world*.

"I Doubt Nothing but the Certainties"

wrote François Villon (born 1431) in his "Ballade du concours de Blois" (also called "Je meurs de soif" and "Ballade des contradictions"). This poem with its many contradictions may strike us as weird and at first glance may even be difficult to understand.

But what is great about it is that its allegedly complicated character fits well in a challenging and painful self-transformation process, here, in particular, the journey from egocentricity to an understanding that every person is a particle of the Universe. But there is precondition to this adventure. Before one can shift a paradigm of thinking, the existence of the pattern itself must be perceived. And this will not happen without questioning, without doubting.

Unfortunately, most of us are trapped in more-or-less comfortable certainties that we don't bother to question. But to challenge what seems to be obvious is one of the first steps that may ultimately lead to discovery. Here is Villon on uncertainties:

> *I die of thirst beside the fountain*
> *I'm hot as fire, I'm shaking tooth on tooth*
> *In my own country I'm in a distant land*
> *Beside the blaze I'm shivering in flames*
> *Naked as a worm, dressed like a president*
> *I laugh in tears and hope in despair*
> *I cheer up in sad hopelessness*
> *I'm joyful and no pleasure's anywhere*
> *I'm powerful and lack all force and strength*
> *Warmly welcomed, always turned away.*

I'm sure of nothing but what is uncertain
Find nothing obscure but the obvious
Doubt nothing but the certainties
Knowledge to me is mere accident
I keep winning and remain the loser
At dawn I say "I bid you good night"
Lying down I'm afraid of falling
I'm so rich I haven't a penny
I await an inheritance and am no one's heir
Warmly welcomed, always turned away.

I never work and yet I labor
To acquire goods I don't even want
Kind words irritate me most
He who speaks true deceives me worst
A friend is someone who makes me think
A white swan is a black crow
The people who harm me think they help
Lies and truth today I see they're one
I remember everything, my mind's a blank
Warmly welcomed, always turned away.

Merciful Prince may it please you to know
I understand much and have no wit or learning
I'm biased against all laws impartially
What's next to do? Redeem my pawned goods again!
Warmly welcomed, always turned away.
The Poems of François Villon, pp. 177-178.

The contradictions used by Villon are to awaken the reader's vigilance and make him wander in thought, questioning, for example, the friendship of somebody who is always fair-spoken and nodding. This may be pleasant, but from something that is obvious there is neither stimulation for questioning, nor spark for creativity. The dogmas given us to believe are to protect that order considered safe by their creators and, indeed, they safeguard the world from the danger of doubting its rules and, by the way, from any heresy.

The Beautiful Uncertainty

Once upon a time there was a young woman who was not able to listen to her inner voice and to trust it. That is why she used to read horoscopes every day, looking for advice. She would do it at work, starting her day by reading the last page of the local newspaper in the office. One day her horoscope informed her that she was to face a reprimand from her supervisor. The moment when she was finishing reading this prediction to her colleagues, the supervisor entered the room, and seeing her in front of a newspaper, made a comment on the inappropriateness of reading during work. "See? Horoscopes never lie," the girl remarked when her boss had left.

Not everybody would share this girl's curiosity when it comes to the events that are to happen to us. Some people would refuse to be deprived of the excitement that comes from not knowing the future. Others do not want to know it because they are afraid of finding out about prospective unlucky news. It might spoil or badly influence the current stream of life of those persons, even if the prophecy would later turn out to be untrue. Yet, there are people who would have concerns regarding what they would hold to be the moral and religious aspects of such revelations.

Let us now take a look at the couple who believed, in contrary to the horoscope girl, that the mutual love that they were experiencing was not captured in "the book of events" as presented in the poem "Love at first sight," by Wisława Szymborska, the Polish poet who won the 1996 Nobel Prize in literature. They believed that what brought them together was "a sudden passion," and were certain about it. The poet, known from her strong devotion and admiration to the phrase "I don't know," writes about the beauty of uncertainty, asking about many possible coincidences when today's lovers might have passed each other on the streets, stairs, building; saw themselves "in some revolving door," issued apology in a crowded passage or called "the wrong number," which in fact had belonged to him or to her. In her words: *chance has been toying with them now for years.* Therefore, should we say that what happened to the lovers was destiny? Not really, Szymborska answers, because what we consider to be a beginning, in fact

> *is only a sequel, after all,*
> *and the book of events*
> *is always open halfway through.*
>
> Wisława Szymborska. *View with a Grain of Sand: Selected Poems*, pp. 197-198.

All events are interconnected in ways we don't always or even usually see, she seems to say here. Therefore, how are things when fully understood? Do we shape the course of events, or are we, rather, the subject of fate's more-or-less cruel jokes? Do we know or not know, and to what extent? And if the answer is "yes," then do we know what awaits us around the corner? Do we believe in the events of life as predictable or as coincidental?

What Does the Unpredictable Have to Do With Freedom?

One of my friends revealed to me her concept of paradise. She is resting in a comfortable armchair, which is sitting on a heavenly meadow. In front of her there is the big screen of a home-theater-style TV set. There is a remote control in her hand and on the screen she is watching the film of her life. She can stop the movie at any time and push the "alternative" button on her remote control. The film immediately takes a different direction, and shows to her what would happen if she had decided to marry Harry instead of Glen, or if she had taken a major in pre-law, or if that particular night she had returned home rather than stayed at her friends' place... There is no limit to the "alternative" buttons. And there is no end to her curiosity about the choices that were never realized: these are choices whose existence she was not even aware of, or which she did not follow up on and convert into her life's reality.

Our choices characterize us. They describe our freedom and make us what we are. Of course there are natural limits to our choices. My decision not to buy a private jet because I have only $750 to spend is not really a choice. As well as my decision to be or not to be a part of the Czech Olympic hockey team really cannot be considered a choice when I am not of the Czech nationality and I cannot play hockey.

Surprisingly, though, there are many more opportunities for making choices than we ever realize. Even in the repressive reality of a totalitarian system, a citizen has a choice to express his dissatisfaction and to protest. The price might be enormous and could be even of the ultimate character, when the system would decide to kill a dissident, but nevertheless, one has a choice (and in most cases chooses not to protest).

The correlations between something certain but simultaneously boring, and between something that is uncertain, but by the same token exciting and maybe risky, is well known. *Running the chance* to the point of *double or nothing* takes a brave or a stupid person. But if one does not take chances, a certain part of one's life remains hidden and silent. To deal with what is unpredictable is our human lot. On how we deal with these uncergtainties, results of a poll taken among a huge sample of eighty-year-old people who were asked about their biggest regrets showed that most of them had regretted not taking a risk, rather than making mistakes in their lives.

The totalitarian political system was mentioned because it did not tolerate the unpredictable. There is a connection between an attitude towards unpredictability and tolerance in a general sense. Tolerance assumes the space for variety, a doubt and an unknown; narrow-mindedness always knows everything better and thus hates surprises.

In the totalitarian system of the Soviet Union, earthquakes, airplane crashes, and mine disasters were not reported—and one of the reasons was of course the fact that they did not fit the image of the perfect system. Another reason was that those events were unpredictable, thus existed beyond the control of the party; and what was beyond its control, had to be sentenced to non-existence. Freedom could not be allowed because it assumed choices.

Oneness claimed by the state, by a political party, or by some other influential organization is not only illusory, but is also dangerous and should be treated as a warning for those who are not in agreement with the united group. Those people will be understood as enemies and as such, in the extreme case, might be physically eliminated.

Of course, not every instance of this "oneness" is a scourge to be avoided at all costs—there is a just war (when we are forced to defend), just persecutions (when we have to isolate those who deprived freedom other people), and proper morality, shared by the majority of religions, called "the natural order." This so-called "natural order" reflects not only the moral principles formulated by the Ten Commandments, but a common sense and pragmatism. Its goal is creation of situation in which one could exercise the maximum of freedom at no cost of others' freedom. The "natural order" through drawing limits to our liberty, help *all* men to exercise their freedom. It teaches us how to be free without depriving others their right to exercise the same liberty. The French Revolution definition of freedom in a very careful way marked the limits of human liberty—freedom is the liberty of doing everything that doesn't harm others. But it means not only not to hurt. It means to respect the others' rights to be free in the same way we are. Live and allow others to live, we are almost inclined to say here. If such a prescription for freedom would prevail, we would live in a much happier world.

Prisoners of Polarity

Many choices that one makes are based on one's value system. If moral choices are rooted in a dualistic way of thinking, they are limited to two options: the selection of goodness or evil. There is no room for a choice of "lesser" evil. One who operates according to this system will never get rid of guilt feelings. One that is imprisoned in polarity will never achieve an internal peace.

In one scene from *Master and Margarita* by Mikhail Bulgakov, which takes place on the roof of one of the Moscow's buildings, there is a confrontation between a young man, Matthu Levi, and Woland, the older man who embodies Satan himself. The Christ's messenger does not greet the Prince of Hell because he despises him. At that point in the story, Woland reminds Levi that he used to be a tax collector—nothing to be proud of, and accuses him of being righteous and blind to existence of shadows between the good and the bad. He poses a question:

> *Would you like to denude the earth of all*
> *the trees and all the living beings in order to satisfy your*
> *fantasy of rejoicing in the naked light? You are a fool.*
> Mikhail Bulgakov, *Master and Margarita*, pp. 367-368.

What Woland meant here is not a moral relativism that erases the border between good and evil (and in fact might be expected from Satan), but the entire field of more abstract concepts that simply need more careful or sophisticated distinctions than a simple binary one. M. Bulgakov, the author of the book quoted, dedicated his work to *Part of that Power which eternally wills evil and eternally works good*, challenging the common ultimate distinction between goodness and evil. The author confronts "the inhuman" disciple of Jesus with an evil, that is compassionate.

In addition to the encounter with Woland, the reader has a chance to observe Matthu Levi's confrontation with the Procurator of Judea, Pontius Pilate. The former hates and holds Pilate in contempt, accusing him of the death of Jesus. The latter, who ordered that Yehudah of Kerioth, the one who betrayed his Teacher, to be killed, tries to explain to Levi (who refuses to accept any help and a gift from Pilate) that hatred expressed by him wouldn't please his master, Yeshua:

> "I know that you consider yourself a disciple of Yeshua, but I can tell you that you did not learn anything of what he taught you. For if you had, you would surely accept something from me. Remember, he said before he died that he blamed no one." Pilate raised his finger significantly, his face was twitching. "And he himself would certainly have accepted something. You are cruel, he was not cruel."
> Mikhail Bulgakov, *Master and Margarita*, p. 342.

Let me return again to language's inadequacy in reflecting shadows that lie between good and bad. When language is given to us, it is given with its categories and rigorous limits. Children are trained from the very beginning to accept the state of absolute truth: "you did it or you didn't do it" they are asked with no room at all for the nature of their intentions. *The path to hell is paved with good intentions* as the saying goes, and we don't want to hear about the child's not wanting to have done what was done. Here, the adult will declare, "So what? You did it, regardless your 'good' intentions." An apt description of the adult way of presenting the world to children through language we find in a fragment of *Memoirs of a Dutiful Daughter* by the French philosopher Simone De Beauvoir. She describes how difficult it was for her to deal with "clear-cut compartments" of thinking and categorizations imposed on her by the adults. Simone had been always forced to distinguish between good and bad, right and wrong, people who deserved be highly admired and those who were worthy of total condemnation: there was no room for any gray area. The girl considered such demands as unreasonable and cruel because she was able to see "grays and half-tones everywhere." The tragic consequence of the necessity to follow adult expectations was that stereotypes and myths won out over the truth, which the girl decided to "dwindle into insignificance."

Is there a way of escape from the cage of polarity? In looking for such a way out of this cage, one has to see and understand beyond the limits created by every dichotomous polarization and go the third way, the way beyond the "either-or" dilemma.

And indeed, why not try to find an extra-systemic solution and turn for a while from the realm of *knowledge*, in which domain we *have to know,* to *feelings*? And why to feelings? Because in the realm of feelings both *yes* and *no, either* and *neither, predetermined* and *unpredictable* are possible at the same time. Such a switch from certainty to uncertainty might open the gate to the universe that operates beyond our logic.

This universe operating beyond our logic is the universe with realities that are not captured or appreciated by this logic, a logic that organizes our conceptual world, disallowing time that is not chronological, space that has many more than three dimensions, and contraries that might not be contradictories but might, rather, co-exist simultaneously—beyond this logic, in other words, that prevents us from losing our distinctiveness and our individuality, and that, finally, prevents us from achieving a profound sense of unification with the surrounding Nature and Cosmos.

Contradictions and a Rain-charmer

Before we enter a gate that leads to the non-contradictory world of unity it is necessary to prepare ourselves. Preparation requires that we build a fresh skin under the old shell of our linguistically-controlled ways of thinking. The new covering, which is not contaminated by an ego-centered poison, creates fundamentals for further self-understanding in which the core feeling is that we are an inseparable part of the universe. To achieve the state in which we would become one of the uncountable, harmonious strings in some cosmic music, we must find peace with ourselves.

To be reconciled with oneself, one needs another human being. As Hungarian-Czech-American existential psychiatrist and psychoanalyst Thomas Hora has written, *To understand himself man needs to be understood by another. To be understood by another he needs to understand the other.*

Only then one may attempt to comprehend oneself. Unfortunately, what is typical for our human condition is a lack of understanding, agreement, and harmony with ourselves, rather than a peace. Luckily for us, nevertheless, sometimes such an internal tension may be a sign of the beginning of a process of a creative transformation that ultimately will lead to reconciliation with ourselves. We could use here the term *positive disintegration*, coined by the psychologist Kazimierz Dąbrowski. This term sounds like an apt bridge between the old conceptual world in which "disintegration" could not be accompanied by a favorable adjective and a new one, in which "inconsistent" expressions are desired, serving as the only way to express the unity of contradictions. But what happens when there is no end to internal conflicts and, on the contrary, these private struggles take a permanent form?

Undoubtedly, their continuing presence will shape our perception of the surrounding world. Lack of agreement with ourselves does not improve our contacts with others. As part of this complication, we are rather reluctant to admit that the cause of our failure in contacts with others is rooted within us, and, does not come from people who surround us, as we would much more readily believe. Such a mechanism, either recognized by one's consciousness or not, leads of course to problems with the outside world.

Let us return to our preparation and let's say that the new skin of our self-perception prevails. What happens then? The state of peace with oneself inspires many fruitful contacts with the outside world. There is an old Chinese story about a province that had been suffering from a drought for a long time. The inhabitants of the region decided to hire a rain-charmer. He arrived to the region and formulated one condition under which he would agree to fulfill the peasants' desire for rain. He demanded first that he would be provided with a place when he could spend three days in complete seclusion. The old bewitcher's wish was fulfilled. At the end of the third day, rain fell. The people, who were happy and grateful, asked the man how he did it. The enchanter explained that for three days he had been trying to put himself into order, knowing that if he would be in peace with himself, then Nature must also be all right and the rain must fall. And he was right.

The balance between the Nature and us has been described in the following way: *Humankind has not woven the web of life. We are but one thread within it. Whatever we do to the web, we do to ourselves. All things are bound together. All things connect.* This quotation, often misattributed to Chief Seattle, is from the scriptwriter, Ted Perry, who nevertheless had the idea right.

In order to find peace with ourselves we have to be able to hear and to listen to our inner voice.

> *What in a human being is the most personal and his own, is simultaneously embracing the whole of mankind and goes beyond a framework of particular cultures and epochs. Modern man in his most personal view of the surrounding world does not differ from a human being existing dozen thousand years ago.*

So wrote Antoni Kępiński in *Poznanie chorego [Knowing the Patient]*, at p. 148. What can be heard from the inner voice is that the opposites presented and discussed in previous chapters, especially in chapter I and II, are artificial.

And that they are responsible for our fragmented view of the world based on categorizing, classifying, and dividing, and that they are not a reflection of our unconsciousness. They result from our adopting communicative patterns.

Our desire for smooth communication with the external world causes us to treat communicative models as independent realities, forgetting that we had once adopted them for their pragmatic value. These patterns have grown on us like a mask that replaces our face. But what makes our contacts with people easier in various pragmatic ways, does not help in our contacts with ourselves.

And what if *Contraria sunt complementa*?

Communicative patterns, which help to classify and to put reality in order, are based on conventions and fixed associational chains. On a deeper level, they are rooted in the conviction that human nature is of a binary character. The traditional polarities include *intellect, intelligence,* and *logic* vs. *instinct* and *intuition, thought, analysis,* and *interpretation* vs. *feeling (compassion), the rigorous* vs. *the spontaneous, the separatist* vs. *the unitive, power* vs. *sensitivity* and *love, conscious awareness* vs. *unconscious energy, action* vs. *stillness,* and *male wisdom* vs. *female understanding*. These effectively prevent us from true contacts with our inner nature that is a mixture of seeming contraries. Fritjof Capra believes that the first sets of features presented in the preceding examples of paired opposites describe our Western culture in contrast with the Eastern:

> *We have favored self-assertion over integration, analysis over synthesis, rational knowledge over intuitive wisdom, science over religion, competition over cooperation, expansion over conservation, and so on.*
> Fritjof Capra, *The Tao of Physics*, p. 8.

Even in our self-analysis we tend to dichotomize, following the example of Sigmund Freud. Donald MacKinnon and Abraham Maslow described the Freudian way of interpretation this way:

> *Freud rested squarely on 19th-century scientific theory in his reductionism, his tendency to analyze, to dissect, to dichotomize ('Aristotelianism'). Presented with a problem, Freud spontaneously and automatically split the field into two or three discrete parts, mutually exclusive, not at all alike in any way, and usually in antagonistic relation to each other, for example, the conscious vs. the unconscious, ego vs. id vs. superego, instinct vs. society, death instinct vs. life instinct.*
> Donald MacKinnon and Abraham Maslow,
> "Personality," in H. Helson, ed.,
> *Theoretical Foundations of Psychology,* pp. 642-643.

And let us ask one more important question: does a single opposite particle truly exist? Not really, we may answer, because what is opposite in nature, cannot exist by itself! It exists only in relation to its opposite as part of a pair. No wonder that the Buddha treats reality in a "relative" way.

Maybe the best-known pair of opposites is *yang* and *yin*. *Yang* is associated with the bright, warm outside; with strong, male creative power, and rational intellect of "heavenly" origin. They are symbolized by the sun and the day it rules, which is loaded with active, positive, and stimulating energy characteristic of life. *Yin,* by contrast, is associated with the dark, cold inside that receives and absorbs, with a receptive, intuitive mind, and with female and maternal substances, characteristics of the earth. Those elements are symbolized by the moon and her daughter—night that is filled with blackness and sadness, passivity and death.

As Capra (*The Tao of Physics*, p. 106) explained it: *"Yin" is the quiet, contemplative stillness of the sage, "yang" the strong, creative action of the king.* Two elements are the extremes but simultaneously they are mutually complementary. Change, so natural and inevitable in our life, comes with a movement of the pendulum of time, that brings back what once was perceived as obscure, and promotes it as fashionable.

Further, according to Capra (at p. 107), *each time one of the two* [opposite] *forces reaches its extreme, it already contains in itself the seed of its opposite.* Hegel, a German philosopher, believed that all our ideas about the world are mortal in sense of their temporality. A just-invented idea, which he called the *thesis*, after a while has to face its opposite, named the *antithesis*. The two, when combined, create a whole, called the *synthesis*. But even the most beloved and perfect notion becomes questionable when it is confronted with its opposite number. In this way, according to Hegel, the *synthesis* turns itself into another *thesis* under the attack of its own *antithesis*. Looking at *yin* versus *yang* or the *thesis* versus the *antithesis* concepts, we might state that there is only one constant thing in this world—change. But is change a *real* change? Have we not learned enough times that there is *nothing new* under the sun? Why? Because instead of perceiving *a totality*, we are constantly involved in *parts*. We and our culture belong to the realm of the intellect, of which, according to Capra, the major function is *to discriminate, divide, compare, measure, and categorize.*

The quoted opposites—*thoughts* versus *feelings,* or *logic* versus *sensitivity*—are artificial opposites and relations between them are more of a supplementary nature. We cannot neglect feelings and sensitivity or our intellect would be sentenced for being one-sided. And a mind suffering from lack of wider perspective is limited. The presence of so-called irrational components is a must in full development of human intellect. Waldemar Szelenberger (in a journal article, "Swiat paranoidalny" or, in English, "Paranoid World") listed three such illogical "fundamental delusions" which direct our mostly-rational activities: a belief in our own immortality, a faith in the unselfish character of human feelings and a confidence in the sense and purposefulness of the universe.

Lack of balance in terms of absence of contrary (but complementary) elements that belong to the inventory of intellect and emotions results in a human being who is not able to achieve inner harmony. For example, the man who rejects in his personality so-called "female elements" like tenderness, interest in children, and showing affections, may become only one-way communicator of power and aggression. A woman who is reduced only to the role of mother, and supposedly lacks ambitions because she is not strong-minded, cannot fulfill herself as a *unity* of contraries. This unity of semantically opposite elements describes Nature, human race, our life, and our death.

The search for the unity of contradictory elements, connections between various disciplines, and universal patterns that may be present in seemingly distant areas of knowledge, have long occupied the human mind. According to Giordano Bruno, the creative activity of the mind consists in the search for the one in the many, for simplicity in variety. The tendency toward creating a summation that would explain in a relatively simple way the mystery of Nature was common for a physicist trying to describe in one equation all phenomena, an alchemist looking for a philosopher's stone, a writer attempting to answer the ultimate question of the purpose of the human condition, an anthropologist who tried to prove universalism of all civilizations, a mystic and an astronomer who were dealing with phenomenon of timelessness. Charles Fort, inspiration of INFO (*International Fortean Organization*) and its journal, pointed out that what was common for wise people of all ages was the attempt to understand the sense of our existence. They differed in their methods examining stars, art, or the economy, but if we believe that a certain fundamental unity of all phenomena prevails at the base of our being, it does not matter where we start our search; in the field of astronomy, economy, or history. Expanding circles can be started from any point whatsoever.

Where Does the Robin's Tail Reside? (From the Perspective of a Grain of Sand)

Let us return to language, that is, to the most imperfect and at the same time the most necessary tool in dealing with the world, especially in terms of sharing our thoughts about it. The poet already quoted, Wisława Szymborska, presents in one of her poems a view from a perspective of a grain of sand. She challenges the reader's common sense by telling him: imagine that you are a sand particle, and that you feel and act like it. Forget the human description of it, its function, shape, and relative location recognized by a human need to locate *oneself* in space and time (as the author of the poem explains, the fact that the wind brought it to the windowsill is just our observation, not its experience). Be yourself, be like a grain of sand, freed from a concept that is rooted in language because:

> *For it, it is no different from falling on anything else*
> *with no assurance that it has finished falling*
> *or that it is falling still.*
>
> Wisława Szymborska, *View with a Grain of Sand: Selected Poems*, p. 136.

The falling down of a grain? Possible? Yes, but only in our Newtonian imagination. In a non-Newtonian, but Einsteinian world, there would be just a peregrination, a wandering of a sand particle. On the other hand, in a non-Newtonian and non-Einsteinian world, it would be motionless. And of course, this affair with a windowsill—its personal nature is something completely overlooked by the onlookers who are describing the particle of sand here!

Szymborska in a merciless way reveals the imperfect nature of human perception. First she puts us into imagining things as if in the shoes (the position and experience) of a grain of a sand, then she undoes our related illusions, reminding us that the objects we perceive are totally uninterested in the opposite process: they are not going to try to be in our shoes!

Let us consider the example of a lake that we might describe in talking of a "a wonderful view of a lake," an example where it may nonetheless be clear to us that the lake itself is quite indifferent to our esthetic delights.

The objects in these various examples are still and peaceful, or alive and vigorous, or non-visible. It doesn't matter, so long as they are themselves. When reading Szymborska's poems we are reminded about the very important ontological fact: what we perceive and declare about the world is only *our interpretation of it*. What we consider "a view" is just our view of it and *the view doesn't view itself:* has no colors, shapes, sounds, smells or feelings:

> *The lake's floor exists floorlessly,*
> *and its shore exists shorelessly.*
>
> Wisława Szymborska, *View with a Grain of Sand: Selected Poems*, pp. 135-136.

Just as in a space where we mark the bark of trees with a white chalk to escape from feeling that we are in the middle of nowhere, we do the same with time, dividing it into intervals, hoping that it will allow us to flee from a lifeless eternity. In this way we create a continuum where it does not exist, an assignable cause where the occurrence is casual and purposeless, and sketch a map of stars, which ceased to exist millions years ago. Yes, we count seconds, the first one, the second, and the third, but how often we do remember that *they're three seconds only for us*. (Wisława Szymborska, *View with a Grain of Sand: Selected Poems*, p. 136.)

We, the users of language have created a world of order. Thanks to this order we obtained a significant power of dividing and ruling. We have the power over other men who are, as we are, enslaved by concepts. We don't, however, have power over a little bird that mocks our imaginary divisions and frontiers.

Oh, the leaky boundaries of man-made states! Szymborska observes in one of her poem helping us to recognize how disobedient are the particles of the nature which disregard the importance of *our order*, and almost ridicule them in a frivolous way. She tells us about the "impunity" of borderless clouds, desert sand or mountain pebbles, and *a humble robin, still, its tail resides abroad while its beak stays home...* Not without sadness, the poet finally declares:

> *Only what is human can truly be foreign.*
> *The rest is mixed vegetation, subversive moles and wind.*
> Wisława Szymborska, *View with a Grain of Sand: Selected Poems*, p. 100.

A bird is one of the most common symbols of freedom. Many of us envy its lightness in moving in space. The birds seem to be free from the bi-polar gravitation. If one might look at the world and himself from the perspective of a robin, one might notice that the opposites are only quasi-contradictory. Such understanding would open a new dimension of perception. In this new dimension one may obtain reconciliation with himself, and harmony with the self will be achieved. A precondition for experiencing a sensation of an ultimate contact with Nature would be fulfilled and one might be ready to transcend oneself.

As the Epilogue that follows immediately suggests, what we need is the fundamental shift in understanding, which will ultimately lead to a more profound honoring of related powerful basic values by which our lives can be guided.

Contact

EPILOGUE: THIS I BELIEVE

I believe in the strength of goodness. The power of deeds that are motivated by the striving for goodness ultimately melt down the most impressive and allegedly the most solidly established empires based on lies, contempt, and injustice. Acts of goodness are supported by their natural allies that consist of four sisters: truth, beauty, dignity, and justice. Each of us carries embryos of all five of these values within us. Through our choices we can either cultivate them or push them aside into the abyss of non-existence, some of whose embers we contain as well.

I believe that goodness radiates and warms distressed people; it also has the power of inspiration. As one should avoid those who are bitter, cynical, and envious because their negativity sneaks into others' hearts, one should seek those whose actions are rooted in compassion, respect for others, and hope.

I believe in the power of love. I believe that in order to observe the commandment of love one should start with oneself. How can one love one's neighbor if not able to love oneself? In order to carry love, to share it, one must have it first. The precondition of giving something is producing it in the first place. It cannot be done without forgiving ourselves. If the baggage we hold is too heavy, it will prevent us from moving on. If I can reconcile with an imperfect self, than I will have enough strength to love others.

I believe that genetic predisposition is not a destiny but is a risk. I believe in the freedom to shape our fate. We have the power of refusing to be a toy of fate. One's responsibility for personal choices, the heroism of admitting mistakes, and the wisdom of learning from mistakes create the basic ingredients of an apt use of the freedom given to us as human beings. *Our weaknesses are not our destiny—the boldness of overcoming them is.*

I believe that every person regardless of origin, race, education, career, or financial situation is an equally important ingredient of the universe, like a drop of water in communicating tubes; each of our actions creates an indelible mark on the network of events. Being a part of others' lives we influence their fate. We can imagine a woman who is considering committing suicide. Being unsure about it, she is looking for a sign that would allow her to make a final decision, and she meets our kind smile. Friendliness of strangers changes her mood. She decides to live. Unintentionally we have saved someone's life. Ten years later the woman who did not commit suicide discovers a cure for cancer.

I believe that the world is heading in the correct direction. The awareness of evils, miseries, human meanness, and regular crises should not obfuscate the obvious truth that there is also the intensification and ongoing increase of tolerance, non-indifference for others' sufferings (including those of entire nations), a concern for nature, and the fight against exploitation, humiliation, and the violating of human rights.

Finally, I believe that the establishing of a fulfilling, inspiring and rewarding contact between two people is possible — I would like to thank my wife, Agnieszka, for helping me to reach this conclusion.

REFERENCES

Adler, Alfred. *The Practice and Theory of Individual Psychology.* Translated by P. Radin. 1925, London: Routledge & Kegan Paul. Revised edition, 1929, same publisher.

Austin, J. L. *How to Do Things with Words.* 1962, Oxford: Clarendon Press.

Bacon, Francis. *The New Organon and Related Writings.* Edited by Fulton H. Anderson. 1960, New York: Macmillan.

Berenstain, Stan, and Berenstain, Jan. *The Berenstain Bears and the Truth.* 1983, New York: Random House.

Berry, John W. "Acculturation as varieties of adaptation," pp. 9-25 in A. Padilla, ed., *Acculturation: Theory, models and some new findings.* 1980, Boulder, CO: Westview.

Blake, William (1757-1827). *There Is No Natural Religion.* (Plate b11: Section VII, Application). 1794-1795; multiple reprints.

Bulgakov, Mikhail. *The Master and Margarita.* Translated by Mirra Ginsburg. 1987, New York: Grove Weindenfeld.

Camus, Albert. *The Plague.* Translated by Stuart Gilbert (1964). 1991, New York: Vintage Books.

Capra, Fritjof. *The Tao of Physics: An Exploration of the Parallels Between Modern Physics and Eastern Mysticism.* Third Edition, updated. 1991, Boston: Shambhala.

Cohen, Leonard. "Light as the Breeze" from *The Future*, 1992. Lyrics published in Cohen, Leonard. *Stranger Music.*

Cohen, Leonard. *Stranger Music. Selected Poems and Songs.* 1993, Toronto: Random House.

Cortazar, Julio. *Hopscotch.* Translated by Gregory Robessa. 1966, New York: Pantheon Books.

Dąbrowski, Kazimierz. *Personnalité, psychonévroses et santé mentale d'après la théorie de la désintégration positive.* 1965, Warsaw: Państwowe Wydawnictwo Naukowe.

Dąbrowski, Kazimierz. *Positive Disintegration.* J. Aronson, editor. 1964, Boston: Little, Brown.

Dąbrowski, Kazimierz. *Psychoneurosis Is Not An Illness: Neuroses and Psychoneuroses From the Perspective of Positive Disintegration.* 1972, London: Gryf Publications.

De Beauvoir, Simone. *Memoirs of a Dutiful Daughter.* 1959/2005, New York: Harper Collins.

Dickinson, Emily (1830-1886). "The Soul Selects Her Own Society" (1862). In *The Complete Poems of Emily Dickenson.* Introduction by Martha Dickinson Bianchi. 1924, Boston: Little Brown.

Diogenes [also Diogenes Laertios, Diogenes Laërtius, Diogenes, Laertes] (fl. 200s CE?). *Lives of Eminent Philosophers.* With an English translation by R. D. Hicks. In two volumes. 1942, London & Cambridge, MA: Harvard University Press.

Dixon, Maria. 1999, personal communication.

Ekai, called Mumon. *The Gateless Gate.* Pp. 83-155 in *Zen Flesh, Zen Bones.* (See entry in this bibliography.)

Fraser, J. T., editor. *The Voices of Time.* 1981, Amherst: The University of Massachusetts Press.

Fort, Charles. *INFO Journal: Science and the Unknown.* [inspiration of INFO, the organization and its journal.]

Fort, Charles. *The Book of the Damned.* 1919, New York: Boni & Liveright, Publishers.

Herzen, Alexander Ivanovich. *From the Other Shore.* At pp. 3-162 (Chapter VI, Omnia Mea Mecum Porto, at pp. 123-142) in *From the Other Shore* and *The Russian People and Socialism.* Translated by Moura Budberg. 1956, London: Weidenfeld and Nicolson. Reprint, 1979, London: Oxford University Press.

Herzen, Alexander Ivanovich. *From the Other Shore.* At pp. 336-469 (Chapter VI, Omnia Mea Mecum Porto, at pp. 442-459) in *Selected Philosophical Works.* Translated by L. Lavrozov. 1956, Moscow: Foreign Languages Publishing House.

Hoffman, Eva. *Lost in Translation: A Life in a New Language.* 1989, New York: D. P. Dutton.

Holmes, Oliver Wendell. Opinion for the U.S. Supreme Court, in the case of Towne v. Eisner, 245 U.S. 418 (1918). Argued Dec. 12, 1917; decided Jan. 7, 2018.

Hora, Thomas. "Tao, Zen and Existential Psychotherapy," *Psychologia [Kyoto, Japan]*, vol. 2 (1959): pp. 236-242.

Janion, Maria. *Wampir. Biografia symboliczna [Vampire. A Symbolic Biography].* 2003, Gdańsk: Słowo/obraz terytoria.

Kapleau, Roshi Philip. *Zen: Dawn in the West.* 1980, Garden City, NY: Anchor Books.

Kapuscinski, Ryszard. "Koniec wieku ["The End of the Century"], conversation with Kapuscinski" by Witold Beres and Krzysztof

Burnetko. *Tygodnik Powszechny,* September 4, 1994, No. 36, pp. 8-9.
Kępiński, Antoni. *Poznanie chorego [Knowing the Patient].* 1978, Warsaw: PZWL.
Korzybski, Alfred. *Science and Sanity: An Introduction to Non-Aristotelian Systems and General Semantics.* Fifth edition. 1995, Forest Hills, NY: Institute of General Semantics.
Kundera, Milan. *The Unbearable Lightness of Being.* Translated by M. H. Heim. 1987, New York: Perennial Library.
Kundera, Milan. *Testaments Betrayed: An Essay in Nine Parts.* Translated by Linda Asher. 1995, New York: Harper Collins.
Lawrence, D. H. (1885-1930). *The Escaped Cock.* Edited by Gerald M. Lacy. 1973, Los Angeles: Black Sparrow Press.
Lechoń, Jan. *Pytasz, co w moim życiu z wszystkich rzeczą główną.* Translated by Marcel Weyland, posted in Roman Antoszewski's blog *Jedno zdumienie dziennie... (One amazement per day...).* October 19, 2006; www.antoranz.net/CURIOSA /ZBIOR6/C0610/20061019-QZM01073_Lechon.HTM.
Lechoń, Jan. *Pytasz, co w moim życiu z wszystkich rzeczą główną.* Translated by Watson Kirkconnell. First published in *A Golden Treasury of Polish Lyrics.* 1936, Winnipeg, Canada: The Polish Press, Ltd; reprinted at p. 111 of *Treasury of Polish Love Poems, Quotations & Proverbs in Polish and English.* 2001, New York: Hippocrene Books.
MacKinnon, Donald W., and Abraham H. Maslow. "Personality." Pp. 602-655 in Harry Helson, editor. *Theoretical Foundations of Psychology.* 1951, New York: D. Van Nostrand.
Maugh, Thomas H. II. "Suprising Survey on Sex: Mild, Not Wild, Is Par," *San Francisco Chronicle,* October 7, 1994, pp. A1 & 9.
Meerloo, Joost A. M. "The Time Sense in Psychiatry." Pp. 235-252 in Fraser, J. T., editor. *The Voices of Time.* 1981, Amherst: The University of Massachusetts Press.
Messer, Stanley B. & Warren, C. Seth. *Models of brief psychodynamic therapy. A Comparative Study.* 1991, New York: Basic Books.
Milne, A. A. *Winnie-the-Pooh.* 1926, New York: E. P. Dutton. Reprinted in A. A. *The Complete Tales of Winnie-the-Pooh.* 1994, New York: Dutton.

Moore, Thomas. *Soul Mates. Honoring the Mysteries of Love and Relationship. 1994,* New York: Harper Perennial.
Mostwin, Danuta. *Testaments: Two Novellas of Emigration and Exile.* 2005, Athens, OH: Ohio University Press.
Ortega y Gasset, José. *The Revolt of Masses.* 1932/1964/1993, New York: W. W. Norton & Co.
Palmer, Helen. "Introduction," in Stuart, Micheline. *The Tarot,* pp. VII-X. (See entry for M. Stuart in this bibliography.)
Porter, Eleanor H. *Pollyanna.* 1913, Boston: L. C. Page & Company.
Potocki, Jan. *Rekopis znaleziony w Saragossie [The Saragossa Manuscript].* In two volumes. 1950, Warszawa: Czytelnik.
Saint-Exupéry, Antoine de. *Le Petit Prince* and its English translation, *The Little Prince.* 1943, New York: Reynal & Hitchcock. *The Little Prince.* 1971, New York: Harcourt Brace & Co.
M. Schlottmann, Małgorzata: see Warchoł-Schlottmann, Małgorzata.
Smirnoff, Yakov. *Smirnoff in Moscow ... Idaho.* 1993, Showtime [TV Series] Production.
Stuart, Micheline. *The Tarot: Path to Self-Development.* 1996, Boston & London: Shambhala.
Süskind, Patrick. *Perfume. The Story of a Murderer.* Translated by John E. Woods from *Das Parfum.* 1986, New York: Alfred A. Knopf.
Szelenberger, Waldemar. "Swiat paranoidalny" ["Paranoid World"], *Psychiatria Polska,* vol. IX, no. 4 (1975): pp. 463-464.
Szymborska, Wisława. *View with a Grain of Sand: Selected Poems.* Translated by S. Baranczak & C. Cavanagh. 1995, San Diego, New York, London: Harcourt Brace.
Villon, François (1431-1463?). *Œuvres completes de François Villon.* 1854, Paris: P. L. Jacob, Bibliophile. Reprint edition, 1970, Nendeln, Lichtenstein: Kraus Reprint. ["Ballade Villon, Je meurs de soif" at pp. 219-220.]
Villon, François (1431-1463?). *Complete Poems.* Translated by Barbara N. Sargent-Baur. 1994, Toronto: University of Toronto Press. ["I Die of Thirst Beside the Fountain" at pp. 243-245.]
Villon, François (1431-1463?). *The Poems of François Villon.* Translated by Galway Kinnell. New Edition. 1982, Hanover, NH: University Press of New England. ["I Die of Thirst Beside the Fountain" at pp. 177-180.]

Yalom, Irvin D. *The Theory and Practice of Group Psychotherapy*. Fourth Edition. 1995, New York: Basic Books.

Warchoł-Schlottmann, Małgorzata (1999). "The disintegrative personality of a Pole in Germany," *Periphery*, no. 4/5 (1999), pp. 31-33.

Watzlawick, Paul. *An Anthology of Human Communication*. 1964, Palo Alto, CA: Science and Behavior Books.

Weisgerber, Johann Leo. *Vom Weltbild der deutschen Sprache [On the Worldview of the German Language]*. 1950, Düsseldorf: Pedagogischer Verlag Schwann.

Wrobel, Janusz. *Language and Schizophrenia*. 1990. Amsterdam & Philadelphia: John Benjamins Publishing Company.

Zen Flesh, Zen Bones: A Collection of Zen and Pre-Zen Writings. Compiled by Paul Reps with transcriptions by Nyogen Senzaki. 1961, Boston & London: Shambala.

ACKNOWLEDGMENTS

I would like to express my gratitude to several people who read fragments of the draft of the manuscript and inspired me later with their comments, suggestions, and inspirational thoughts. I would like to mention them in an alphabetical order: Marija Dixon, Anna Kaminska, Katarzyna Kietlińska, Bolesław Klimaszewski, the dearest friend who is not among us any more, Halina Massalska, Sylvia Meloche, Jan Palarczyk, Klaus Schlottmann, Małgorzata Warchoł-Schlottmann, Ewa Thompson, and Urszula Wróbel.

My special thanks to Andrei Ciortan, a photographer, who generously allowed me to use several fruits of his art in the book.

I am especially indebted to my editor, Mitchell Ginsberg, who has done a tremendous job as a very meticulous, knowledgeable, and academically-oriented literary reviser.

I would like to thank the following for formal permission to quote passages used in this book:

"I Doubt Nothing But the Certainties" from *The Poems of Francois Villon*, translated by Galway Kinnell. Copyright © 1965, 1977 by Galway Kinnell. Reprinted by permission of Houghton Mifflin Harcourt Publishing Company. All rights reserved.

"Lost in Translation" by Eva Hoffman. Copyright © 1989 by Eva Hoffman. Used by permission of Dutton, a division of Penguin Group (USA) LLC.

"Soul Mates" by Thomas Moore. Copyright © 1994 by Harper Collins Publishers.

"The Storm" (cartoon) by Joe Martin. Copyright © 1995 by Neatly Chiseled Features—Mister Boffo.

www.ingramcontent.com/pod-product-compliance
Lightning Source LLC
Chambersburg PA
CBHW031635160426
43196CB00006B/429